CONNECTICUT'S FIFE AND DRUM TRADITION

A

DRIFTLESS CONNECTICUT

SERIES BOOK

This book is a 2011 selection in the Driftless Connecticut Series, for an outstanding book in any field on a Connecticut topic or written by a Connecticut author.

Connecticut's Fife & Drum Tradition

JAMES CLARK

WESLEYAN UNIVERSITY PRESS
Middletown, Connecticut

Wesleyan University Press
Middletown CT 06459
www.wesleyan.edu/wespress

Manufactured in the United States of America

The Driftless Connecticut Series is funded by the
Beatrice Fox Auerbach Foundation Fund
at the Hartford Foundation for Public Giving.

Wesleyan University Press is a member of the Green Press Initiative.
The paper used in this book meets their minimum requirement for
recycled paper.

Library of Congress Cataloging-in-Publication Data
Clark, James.
Connecticut's fife & drum tradition / James Clark.
p. cm. — (Driftless Connecticut series) (Garnet books)
Includes bibliographical references.
ISBN 978-0-8195-7141-0 (cloth : alk. paper) —
ISBN 978-0-8195-7142-7 (e-book)
1. Fife and drum corps—Connecticut—History.
2. Fife and drum corps music—Connecticut—History
and criticism. I. Title. II. Title: Connecticut's fife and
drum tradition.
ML1311.7.C7C53 2011
784.8'4283309746—dc22 2010054058

5 4 3 2 1

CONTENTS

ACKNOWLEDGMENTS

This book is very much a history of my extended family, for the fifers and drummers of the Northeast have been a family to me. I would like to thank Paul Cormier for his friendship and for the endless string of drum corps stories and history that he has related to me during many a late night that turned too soon into dawn. I also owe a great deal to the late Ken Lemley, whose love of music and of drumming never faded throughout the trials of age and sickness. And I would like to thank the members of the Connecticut Valley Field Music, who have allowed me to experiment with ideas about historical performance practice and maintained my interest in the fife and drum through their dedication and friendship.

I would not have become a drummer without the dedication of my mother, Madeline Clark, who listened to countless hours of drumming practice when I was young, and who drove me all around Connecticut so that I could participate in fifing and drumming events in the 1960s. And I am always grateful for the support of my aunt, Rita Clark, who has always provided a refuge where I could think and make music, and whose love of East Hampton and its history are second only to her love for her family.

Sally Rothenhaus, fifer with the Connecticut Valley Field Music, volunteered to manage much of the work involved in creating the illustrations in the book. She has done a superb job and has been an indispensable part of this project.

Lastly, I would like to thank Professor Herbert Arnold of Wesleyan University, whose broad historical perspective, detailed knowledge, and artful polemics have served as a lofty intellectual model for all my own small efforts.

INTRODUCTION

In the fall of 1963, nearing my ninth birthday, I was given a purple-inked, bureaucratic form offering me a choice among musical instruments that I could choose to study in East Hampton's public school music program. I have no idea why I chose the snare drum, but I did. This set in train a series of events that has largely shaped my subsequent experience. No sooner, it seemed, had I begun my lessons than my Aunt Rita took me to meet an elderly gentlemen, a retired postal worker named Tom Hyde, who had been an active drummer throughout most of his life in our local fife and drum corps. Mr. Hyde had a strange drum pad contraption on which he showed me his repertoire of rudiments and beatings: the "pad" was a rather low carpenter's sawhorse. The top board of this sawhorse was upholstered on each end, like the arm of a stuffed chair. The two drummers thus sat facing each other, tapping away quietly, and not ruining anyone's furniture, both aspects of drumming, I have since learned, much appreciated by family members of drummers.

Tom's paraphernalia also extended to several pairs of drumsticks completely unlike anything I had seen in my school band. At my regular lessons in school we all had drumsticks made by one of the large Midwest firms (Slingerland, or more frequently, Ludwig) made from rather bland white hickory and stamped with standard sizes and a company logo. But Tom's sticks resembled the work of a fine cabinetmaker rather than a factory product. Made out of rare woods I had never seen, their lines were smoothly flowing, with a long and gradual taper, and finished to a soft and extraordinarily smooth sheen. Some of the sticks were made of rosewood, which had a dark red hue veering toward black as the sticks aged. Others were jet-black (and very heavy) ebony. But the most beautiful of all were the ones Tom called snake wood, with a very pronounced grain that reminded me of pictures I had seen of tigers. All of these sticks, I was told, were made in the earliest decades of the twentieth century, some earlier. Tom gave me a pair of his rosewood sticks, and I still use them occasionally in parades and concerts.

After my lesson, Tom would take out his pride and joy, the drum he had marched with for decades. I understood it to be a drum made by Eli Brown, a name all Connecticut drummers were taught to venerate, and the drum was nearly as old as the American republic that it was built to celebrate. Like Tom's drumsticks, this drum was completely unlike the kinds of drums we learned about in school. It was huge; now I think it must have had about an eighteen-inch head and was probably eighteen to twenty inches deep, which with its counterhoops would have made a drum almost two feet tall, which will look large to a slightly shorter than average nine-year-old. The shell was made of richly figured maple, stained and waxed to a soft, dark glow. An old, precariously frayed piece of rope (probably hemp or linen) was threaded through holes in the counter hoops, and ran through pieces of leather that could be adjusted to tension the calfskin heads, which were of that beautiful soft white color and texture that is so distinctive. The contrast with the school's chrome-plated, logo-bedecked, plastic-headed drums could not have been more dramatic.

But Tom Hyde was not a collector; he was a drummer. As we sat on the opposite sides of that sawhorse, he tried to show me the rudiments (in both senses) of the kind of "Ancient drum corps drumming" that he knew. I can still blush when I think of what a hopeless student I must have been. But—and after all these years, I still detect a defensiveness as I say this—nearly everything Tom Hyde showed me was at best foreign or at worst contradictory to the way I had been taught in school.

In school I had been taught that reading standard rhythmic notation was the fundamental process for learning. A normal, moderate tempo I learned to associate with quarter notes. Notes that went twice as rapidly were eighths. Double the speed again, and we had sixteenths. And so forth. I also learned that one played "from the wrist" and that the arms stayed nearly motionless. Well, Tom Hyde appeared never to have heard about quarter notes or eighth notes. He tried to teach me with a system of onomatopes, or mnemonic syllables that I was supposed to memorize and repeat to myself as I drummed out the rhythms. And he employed a kind of motion that involved a loose swinging of his upper arms, quite in contradiction to the demure and restrained movements I had been taught.

The Long Roll, Tom taught, was also called the mama-dada; each bisyllabic parental designation represented two strokes with each hand. As I recall, the distaff side was the left, the paternal the right. Similarly, the flam was a term slowly pronounced ("faa-Lamm") and did approximate the sound of a light grace note preceding an accent. The paradiddle consisted of four strokes, the first (or first two) accented; the "diddle" represented two light taps with the same hand. Roll the "r" at the beginning of ratamacue, and you will know all that can usefully be said about the sound of that rudiment.

I don't think that I absorbed anything very specific from the few lessons Tom Hyde gave me. But more than forty years later I still remember the extraordinary nature of those encounters. I had never seen an adult play music in a home. Music lessons were for children. Yet here was this slim, white-haired, grandfatherly figure eagerly pulling out his sawhorse practice pad and exhorting me so energetically on the correct execution of rolls and paradiddles. Similarly, in my home we certainly didn't have antiques or handmade items, except my grandfather's Parker side-by-side 16 gauge, which I was forbidden to touch. The drum and sticks Tom showed me suggested a whole other world of artisanship and a kind of historical continuity with the early days of New England and the United States that a boy already fascinated by American history found irresistible.

The first summer that I was drumming, 1964, my Aunt brought me to hear the drum corps at the Deep River muster. I may have seen the occasional drum corps in our local Memorial Day parade in East Hampton, but the local area corps had fallen into a kind of dormancy in the late fifties and sixties, and I had no idea what awaited me.

Driving from East Hampton to Deep River is one of the beautiful short drives in Connecticut. Routes 148 and 151 are to this day lovely, winding roads lined with trees and vegetation. In some places, the Connecticut River is visible through the foliage, and the overhanging trees provide shade throughout the day all summer long. During World War II, my mother, then a high school girl, used to bicycle down these roads to visit friends in Deep River. I can't imagine a lovelier place to spend a summer day. As my Aunt Rita drove me down this picturesque route, I learned, as I recall, that nearly every town had a drum corps. We began our drive of course, in East Hampton, home of the East Hampton fife and drum corps (founded 1886). We then went through the periphery of Moodus (home of the Moodus Drum and Fife Corps, founded 1860). As we approached East Haddam (of which Moodus is a part), the Connecticut River was visible through the trees, and we crossed over the famous swinging bridge that allows large boats to move north up the river. On the other side of the river we were in Higganum (Higganum drum corps, founded 1890) and then we entered Chester (org. 1868), which abuts Deep River (corps founded in 1873).

In Deep River, I saw for the first time literally hundreds of people dressed in something resembling historical costume (in the 1960s, historical authenticity was much less exacting than it has become). The festivities I saw before the parade started were an event in themselves. Traditionally, the fifers and drummers would park their cars up at Devitt Field, the local baseball diamond, and walk down Main Street to the beginning of the parade. The variety of cocked hats, tailcoats of eighteenth-century style, workmen's waistcoats, jabots, cravats and other neckwear, leather leggings, knee-breeches, shiny colonial-era shoe buckles, and people of every age, it seemed, from boys and girls barely larger than the drums they played to elderly figures for whom parading in the July sun seemed a very parlous activity, the occasional woman wearing a colonial gown, all present in such a confused profusion made an indelible impression. At noon, all marchers were finally assembled up at the north end of Main Street, and the parade began.

That was the only year I watched the Deep River parade in its entirety. Every year since I have been a participant. What an event it was! Five or six dozen drum corps came down the street, one after the other. In the Deep River parade there are no politicians pandering for votes, no fire engines blasting sirens, not even any Boy Scout or Girl Scout troops waving to their parents: only fife and drum corps. In recent years, some other musical units have been invited, fife and drum corps from Switzerland, Irish flute bands, and a few bagpipe bands. But the parade is really a celebration of traditional American fife and drum music. There are junior corps, in which all the members are under eighteen or twenty-one years of age. There are groups in which the median age approximates that of a retirement community. There are groups that are gaudily made up with uniforms costing thousands of dollars, although this is extremely rare. Some groups are musically much more sophisticated than others. After the parade, each group performs for a few minutes in concert for the other participants and the spectators. The rule at the muster (sometimes only grudgingly observed by those who consider themselves the musical elite) is that each group, be they ever so grand or ever so humble, is given five to eight minutes to make its presentation. This usually eventuates in a full afternoon of music, often ending only as dusk gathers in the river valley.

A most curious and singular part of the day's festivities follows this formal presentation of each corps. The jollification is a semichaotic playing session in which the standard repertory of the American fife and drum (a canon constantly challenged by changing fashion within the community) is played, more or less continuously, into the early hours of the morning (and sometimes the not so early hours—while in recent years I have greatly curtailed my jollifying, I do have recollections of driving home well after sunrise from some of these events).

What is this tradition of fifes and drums in Connecticut? From whence does it derive, what type of people and institutions have made it a continuing part of Connecticut's cultural tradition, and what are its prospects in the future? These are the questions I consider in this book.

CONNECTICUT'S FIFE AND DRUM TRADITION

1 ORIGINS OF THE FIFE AND DRUM

THE EARLY COLONISTS were not Americans but adventurers, pioneers, sometimes outcasts from Europe, establishing settlements in a new, vast, and strange land. Familiar customs and folkways provided continuity and reassurance for colonists isolated from their homes in Europe. Both the fife and the drum were simple to make from materials ready to hand, and were easy instruments on which to play the rustic music of the common people. Unlike the stories of more complex and refined instruments, the history of the fife and drum is very much the story of a folk tradition, of common people making music together as a way to celebrate their successes and to unite them in their struggles. In times before mass communication and the commercialization of popular culture, the gradually evolving tradition of folk music repertory and performance practice was the province of generations of amateur and part-time musicians who kept alive the music of their culture and adapted it to the needs of their own times. As our story progresses, we will see how the fife and drum came to be identified with specifically American values and traditions. But their original use in New England was as a reminder of their European home, and so it is in Europe that our story properly begins.

Two separate but complementary traditions in medieval Europe led to the development of the fife and drum as we know them. During medieval times, the pipe and tabor combination was used throughout much of Europe, sometimes in a military setting, but most often to make dance music. The military fife and drum, which originated in Switzerland, probably in the fourteenth century, were developed as a consequence of cultural contact with the Islamic world during the period of the Crusades. In both these

The Totentanz, or Dance of Death, is a common medieval artistic representation, a reminder of life's transience. In this miniature sculpture, skeletons are playing a pipe and tabor. Courtesy of the Historisches Museum Basel; photographer HMB P. Portner

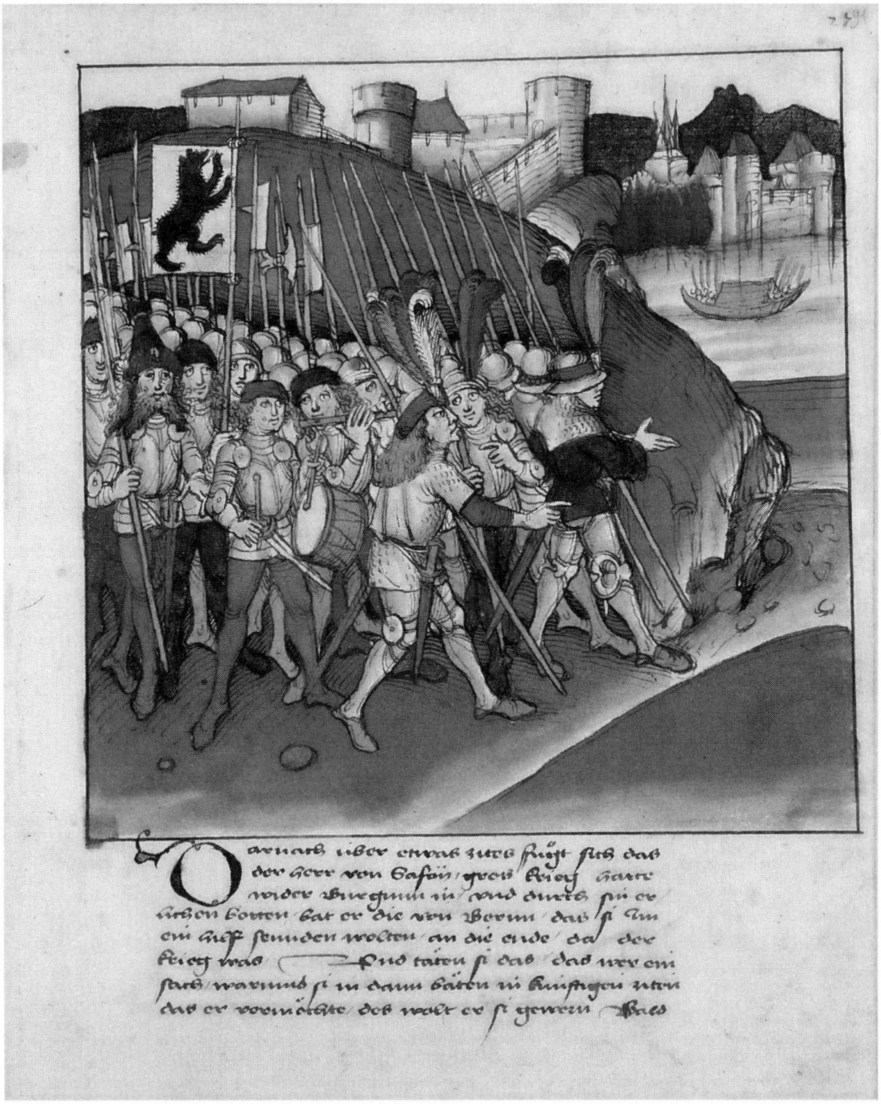

This medieval painting of Swiss soldiers shows a rope tension field drum, not unlike those used in Connecticut's fife and drum corps to this day. Photo courtesy of Burgerbibliothek Bern, Switzerland, Mss.h.h.I.16, p. 91

traditions, the breadth of social function of the fife and drum were established early, for this set of instruments has always been used both for entertainment and relaxation (continued by the pipe and tabor players into the early twentieth century) and for creating the music of war (the Swiss fifers and drummers were renowned as both a civic tradition in several parts of the country and were exported as the very model of what military music should be). A close look at the fife and drum and the uses to which they were put will provide a framework for understanding these instruments as they have come to be used in more modern times.

The Drum

Two types of drum are relevant to our story. In medieval Europe, a small drum called a tabor was used to accompany dancers. The tabor was often played with only one hand, while the other hand fingered a pipe. In medieval paintings taborers can be seen drumming while knights in armor prepare to joust or engage in battle, but they were also used to accompany dancers, and this dual use characterizes our instruments throughout their history: the pomp and ceremony of the military is always being tempered by the unbuttoned ribaldry of the festive celebration and the intimacy of the dance. The other type of drum is the field drum, a larger drum played with a much more intricate technique, which seems to have developed in the fourteenth century in Switzerland.

Drums are called membranophones because their sound is produced by causing a membrane (the drumhead) to vibrate. The essential parts are the head, the shell (which amplifies the sound and controls or alters the timbre of the head) and the tensioning mechanism: a cord or rope laced in a diagonal pattern through wooden counterhoops that when pulled taut, or braced, by leather thongs (often called ears or tugs) pulls the head tight against the shell. The head is struck with a hand or stick, and this is one of the simplest forms of drumming. On some early drums, the head is attached directly to the shell. The normal military drum employs a flesh hoop: a wooden ring around which the edge of the head is tucked. As the rope is tensioned, the counterhoops pull against the flesh hoop, tightening the drum evenly.

The tabor was a small two-headed drum, tensioned with cord, and with a snare or snares often stretched across the top head. Snares are thin cords pulled taut across the head of the drum that vibrate when the drum is struck. A drum with snares is, generally speaking, louder in any given musical situation than a drum without snares. The idea of the snare seems to have come from Turkish drumming. The first time I played with a group of Turkish drummers, I was surprised to see a playing technique that suggests the snare effect. While the right hand strikes the drum with a stick, the stick in the left hand rests lightly against the head, buzzing like a snare. Some Turkish drums also have snares stretched across the head, just like a European snare drum.

While the tabor was a precursor to the military field drum in its construction and use, the direct line of descent is found not in the British Isles but among the medieval burghers and mercenaries of Switzerland. instruments that resemble the classic field drum were probably being used in Switzerland as early as the 1300s. The Swiss field drum is, in all of its essentials, simply a large tabor that is always equipped with snares. By the sixteenth century, there were field drums more than twenty inches in diameter with about the same depth. But if the instrument itself was not much of a departure, the playing techniques that developed to complement the evolving military tactics of the time clearly were. The image of the medieval knight riding into battle heavily armored, mounted on a great, caparisoned charger was becoming anachronistic by the turn of the fifteenth century. Increasingly, large groups of commoners, fighting as foot soldiers in disciplined groups, were able to defeat the mounted and armored noblemen. Perhaps the most famous battle in English history, Henry V's defeat of the French at Agincourt in 1415, was a harbinger of the new tactics. Severely outnumbered by the mounted and armored French nobility, the English archers, commoners to a man, rained down a hail of armor-piercing arrows on the French and won a decisive victory with very little loss of English life. The use of massed foot soldiers increased as this tactic was refined throughout the late medieval and Renaissance periods, largely by the Swiss mercenaries who were retained by many of the wealthy states of Europe. As infantry tactics were based on precision and disciplined action, the Swiss field drums became crucial in communicating orders to the troops. The drums needed to be heard above the din of battle, so they became much larger. A playing technique developed that required the drummer to wield large drumsticks and use both hands almost equally in a series of patterns that were unique to European field drumming.

The hallmark of this style is the unique left-hand stick grip, which iconographic evidence suggests was in place by the fourteenth century, and the system of rhythmic patterns known as rudimental drumming, still practiced in modified form today. The drum or tabor is carried on a sling around the neck or over the right shoulder and sits at an acute angle, the left side of the drum much higher than the right. Because of this angle, the left hand holds the stick in the crook between thumb and forefinger, the palm facing the player, while the right-hand stick is grasped in some variation of a more natural hammer grip. In most of the oldest explanations of this drumming style available to us, the right hand takes the naturally accented beats and is clearly used as the dominant hand. The drummers developed impressive dexterity as the style developed, and by the seventeenth century, at the latest, they were creating a system of alternating the hands (referred to as sticking), playing one or two taps in succession with each, and varying the power and speed of the taps to produce highly organized patterns that could be combined at will in order to create rhythmic phrases. These musical patterns became known as the rudiments of drumming and formed the foundation for all military drumming throughout the succeeding centuries.

Although much of the repertory of the early Swiss field music is lost, the early style of drumming that was based on the rudimental system clearly developed into the military drumming of Europe. From early days, European military drumming has relied on groups of drummers playing in strict unison, and the rudimental system created a reasonably uniform technique and a repertory of rhythmic patterns, making the drumming intelligible and precise. Phrases, or beatings, made up of an orderly succession of these rudiments were easy to memorize and play in unison. A late seventeenth-century English source mentions some rudiments by name. Allowing for the vagaries of English orthography, these are the same names I use in teaching my drum students today, four hundred years later: the "'flam,' 'dragge,' 'roofe,' 'diddle' and . . . 'rowle'" (*New Grove Dictionary of Music* 1980, 5:657).

The fundamental rudiment is the drum roll (or rowle), sometimes called the drummer's long tone. A roll is played by alternating either single strokes (left, right, left, right) or double strokes (left, left, right, right) and speeding up until the individual taps are no longer distinct and the sound is perceived as continuous. The flam is a rudiment that decorates a single beat. The hands play in rapid succession, both loudly. The resulting effect is like a little explosion, an effect preserved in the contemporary European rudiment the *coup de charge*. The paradiddle is a four-note pattern of equally spaced taps, with the sticking left, right, left, left, or the reverse, right, left, right, right. The first two taps are accented; the latter two are quite soft. This pattern illustrates one of the basic ideas of the rudiments. A rudiment normally has three component parts: rhythm, sticking, and accent. In learning to play rudiments correctly, the student learns precise rhythm, control of common sticking patterns, and control of dynamics (or volume).

The elements of accent and rhythm help the drummer place the rudiments into a meter, or pattern of stressed and unstressed beats, which is closely related to poetic meter. For instance, the seven-stroke roll, a very common rudiment, consists of six soft taps followed by an accented stroke.

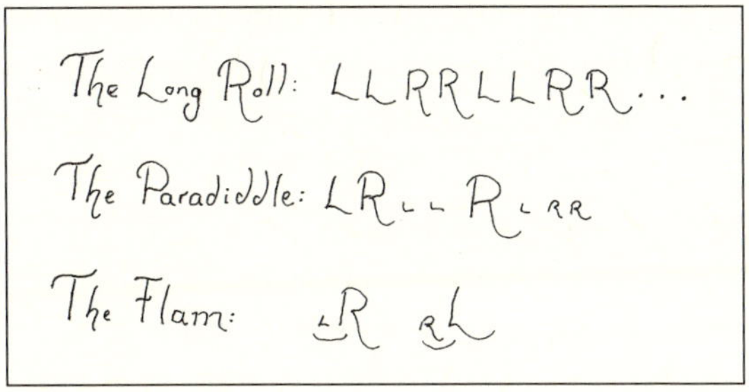

This is the way field drumming has been taught for centuries. Each pattern, or rudiment, is written out in shorthand, and the student learns the details of execution from the teacher. Photo courtesy of Sally Rothenhaus

This rudiment normally begins before the accented beat of the meter such that the last (accented) stroke of the roll lands on the beat, which coincides with the marching step of the music. The paradiddle, however, is stressed at its beginning and finishes with soft taps. The paradiddle nearly always begins on an accented beat within the meter and is always followed by some other rudiment or stroke so that the strong beats within the meter are emphasized.

A strain, or stanza, normally consists of sixteen steps; each left step is slightly accentuated. A drummer familiar with the conventions of the rudiments and marching meter can easily create a beating to accompany tunes or to provide a marching cadence. Of course, if these patterns are followed with complete rigidity, the beatings will be completely uninteresting. Much of the skill of a "rudimental" drummer lies in knowing how to vary the rudiments within each strain.

The Fife

Frequently, a tabor player tapped his drum with a stick held in one hand while blowing a pipe and fingering it with his other. The pipe was often a simple end-blown woodwind with three finger holes. This medieval instrument provides a simple example of how woodwind instruments make music. Musical sound can be described physically as the controlled vibration of air. Every instrument has to create and control vibration, and the pipe does it this way: blowing into a narrow tube concentrates the air stream, increasing its velocity in the same way that a body of water will flow more rapidly if forced down a confining channel. The medieval pipe is of a variety known as the fipple flute; the fipple is a kind of mouthpiece with a narrow opening for the player's breath to enter the bore, or inside column, of the instrument. The air column, if carefully controlled, reaches a consistent velocity of vibration that we recognize as a musical pitch. The length of the tube determines the pitch; a longer pipe produces a slower vibration (lower pitch), and a short pipe produces a more rapid vibration (higher in pitch). The finger holes act as a way of altering the pipe's length. Thus, four different pitches can be played by a pipe with three finger holes.

But the story is more complex and interesting than this. The octave phenomenon describes an especially relevant acoustical property of pitch. Any vibrating body (whether a string, an air column, or a solid object like the bar of a marimba) actually vibrates at several different frequencies at once. (Perhaps the easiest way to understand this is to pluck, quite firmly, the lowest string of a guitar. You can see that the string vibrates in sections.) The fundamental pitch is produced by the sound wave that moves the entire length of the column. Shorter sections of that column vibrate in mathematically regular ratios within that basic vibrating length. For instance, each half of the wave also vibrates exactly twice as fast (since it is half the length), and this more rapid vibration blends so smoothly with the principal tone that people recognize the relationship between them as being nearly identical. This is what we call the interval of the octave. If you touch the string of a guitar lightly at a point exactly in the middle of its vibrating length and release it immediately while plucking it with your other hand, the string will vibrate in two halves, creating a sound just one octave higher than the full length of the string. On the pipe, this octave leap is produced by carefully increasing the velocity of the air supply (most easily by simply blowing harder). In this way, the player can make the instrument leap an octave without changing the fingering, a technique called overblowing.

All woodwinds abide by the same acoustical principles, but each instrument has characteristics that offer specific advantages and problems. The medieval pipe was well suited for its purposes. The fipple flute requires no special skill to master. (It is essentially a simpler version of the recorder schoolchildren use in learning to play simple tunes.) The ability to play it with one hand and a tabor with the other means that one person can serve as a dance band. But having only three finger holes limits the range of available notes. And a fipple is always rather quiet. For these reasons, among others, it was gradually replaced by the transverse flute. The design of this versatile instrument is such that the player holds it extending to the side and blows *across* a hole rather than *into* a mouthpiece. The result is much greater volume, range of pitch, and variety of tone color than a fipple flute can produce. During the Renaissance, the transverse flute became increasingly popular.

The fipple flute (right) is a quiet, end-blown woodwind, like a recorder. The transverse-blown fife (left) is much louder, for outdoor use, and can be heard above the sound of drum. Photo courtesy of Sally Rothenhaus

During the sixteenth century, it was common to build a whole family, or consort, of instruments all of the same design in varying sizes; thus their ranges varied while all approximated the same tone color. Viols and recorders are the best known consort instruments. But people also built transverse flutes of different sizes, and the fife was one of these. It is essentially a Renaissance flute that is very small and thus higher in pitch. Outdoors, particularly when accompanied by large drums during military maneuvers, a very loud instrument is much more useful than a quiet one, whatever refinements the quieter one may possess. Accordingly, the fife was generally given a narrower bore than a flute in order to facilitate overblowing, resulting in a loud, shrill sound. Principally because of the fife's small bore, its lowest, or first, octave is much quieter and smoother in tone than the overblown second octave. In the third octave, the fife's tone is painfully shrill when played in a confined space. In Renaissance times, the fife was used with the Swiss military drum and was sometimes even called the Swiss fife (Schweitzerpfeifen).

Then, late in the seventeenth century, for reasons that remain mysterious, some flute makers in France created a flute in which the bore of the instrument was tapered, so as to be larger close to the blow hole, which solved many of the flute's problems, making the tone more homogeneous throughout its range, and aiding in intonation. A seventh finger hole, operated with a lever (a "key") was also added to the flute, further aiding in intonation and tone production. The increasingly complex instrumental music of the Baroque Age required these technical refinements; the new flute quickly supplanted the recorder in most musical ensembles and completely eclipsed the old-fashioned straight-bore flutes of the Renaissance. Reading musical notation was a gentleperson's accomplishment, as was knowledge of harmony. The baroque flute could only be designed and built by highly skilled instrument makers, and assumed a sophisticated musical sensibility in the player. But European society was highly stratified, and access to sophisticated artistic developments was limited to the privileged classes or the artisans they employed. The common soldiers of the age were generally poor and uneducated men, and such refinements were unavailable to them. These men continued to play the fife (which had not been altered), and so it became associated with simple folk tunes and military signals, the outdoors, and loud, raucous, unrefined music.

We have very few examples of early fifes, and not too clear an idea of what fifers played. They probably played dance tunes and military calls from a much more rough-and-ready folk music tradition than the one that refined musicians mastered. Some of these folk tunes found their way into the written music of the day, arranged and harmonized for keyboard instruments or viols. From these arrangements we can sometimes glean hints as to the sound of the fife in its earliest English usage. According to the earliest accounts, the fifers in the early days of military music simply improvised melodic fragments, rather than complete tunes with regular phrases. This is only possible when a single fifer is playing, and this tradition is remarkably similar to the process we can see in the African-American fife and drum tradition, popularized in recent years by the recordings of Othar Turner especially. The merest skeleton of a tune is repeated and varied above a similarly repetitive but improvisationally varied drum beat. The tunes and drum beats of Turner's style are surely quite different from those of Elizabethan England, but the improvisational character of Turner's music I think can teach us quite a bit about the character of the Elizabethan.

Although we don't know what specific tunes were played, the styles available to the early fifers are pretty well understood. From the earliest dated fife manuscripts and publications throughout the history of the instrument, fifers have drawn heavily on regional dance music traditions to create the repertory of their instrument. In the sixteenth century, this would have meant dances like the branle, the pavane, and the galliard, of which we have many examples, as printed music began to be produced in the early sixteenth century. With the democratization of printing that took place in the late seventeenth century, music publications (as well as books, pamphlets, journals, and newspapers of every sort) became affordable for people of modest means. Among the crush of new material were music books of simple folk tunes and dance music. The most famous of these was *Playford's Dancing Master*, first published in 1651, consisting of 105 tunes suitable for country dancing and directions for the dance steps. The book does not specify that the tunes were to be played on the fife (the title page promises *"Directions for Dancing and Country-Dancing, with the tunes to each dance, for the treble violin"*), but most of these tunes are eminently playable on the fife. They give a clear idea of the types of music that were current in England at the time of the Puritan settlements of New England. Indeed, Playford's book, by providing a repertory for dances and other festive gatherings, encouraged exactly the kind of lewd behavior the Puritans were endeavoring to escape.

Most of these tunes are fairly simple to play, but they show some interesting variety that seems to have been lost in much of the more recent music associated with the fife. Without becoming unduly technical, I will try to explain some of the interesting points of this music. The salient concepts here are (1) phrase length and (2) the concept of mode or key. With just a little bit of musical background, these extremely useful concepts are easily understood.

Modes

Tunes are typically made by using the notes within a particular scale, or key (not really synonymous terms). There are several types of scales, more correctly called modes, in the European tradition. To understand some of the important characteristics of these various modes, first, find the note C on a keyboard. Starting on this C, play the consecutive white notes (or naturals), moving from left to right. You will recognize the familiar sound of the major scale: do, re, mi, fa, sol, la, ti, do. Notice that black keys are located between most of the white ones, except between E and F and between B and C. These

Modes. These are the four types of scale on which most of our traditional fife tunes are based. Photo courtesy of Sally Rothenhaus

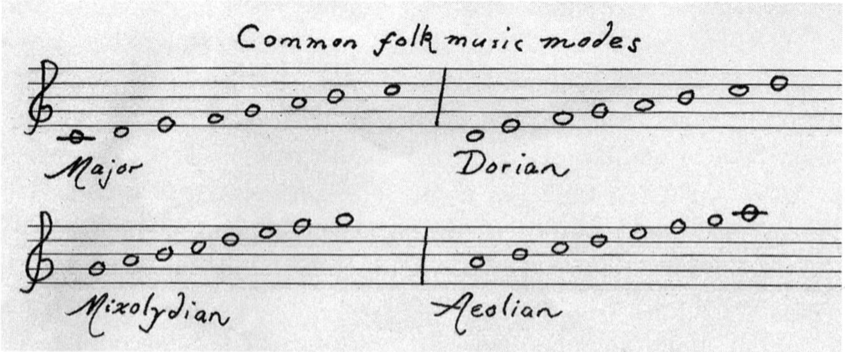

steps without the black keys between them are called half steps, or semitones, because the rate of increase in frequency is half that of the intervals between the other notes (the black notes provide the intervening half steps when they are needed). From this you can see that a major scale includes some notes that are closer together than others (mi-fa and ti-do). The difference between these half steps and the whole steps surrounding them has a strong influence on the character of the music that is made with the scale.

Now, instead of beginning your scale on C, shift it up one key and begin on D instead (D, E, F, G, A, B, C, D). The scale now sounds quite different because the half steps occur between the second and third notes, and then between the sixth and seventh notes. This mode is called the Dorian, and it has long been recognized as having a different character from the major scale (the Ionian mode). Applying the same logic, you can start on any of the white notes, use each successive white note ascending (left to right on the keyboard) and you will notice that the same sequence of half steps and whole steps is never repeated by starting on any two notes.

This is important! Each starting note has its unique pattern of whole and half steps. No two are the same. By the middle of the nineteenth century, most fife tunes were based on the major scale (the one that, in our example, starts on C). But the earlier music gives no privileged position to major-key tunes. The most common other scales or modes were those based on D (Dorian), A (Aeolian), and G (Mixolydian). In addition, many tunes did not adhere rigidly to any particular mode, and the sixth and seventh scale steps, in particular, can often shift by a half step back and forth within a single tune. While a thorough discussion of modal music would be very complex, this explanation will help to understand more fully much of the repertory a fifer usually encounters.

121 Ginnie pug *or* Strawberries and cream

The first tune, "Ginnie Pug," or "Strawberries and Cream," is composed of two regular phrases, the first of four bars, the second of eight. Both phrases are mostly in G minor. The first phrase uses the raised sixth scale degree associated with the Dorian mode (the E natural); the second uses the minor sixth of the Aeolian mode (the E flat). From The Complete Country Dance Tunes from "Playford's Dancing Master," *edited by Jeremy Barlow. Copyright 1985 by Faber Music Ltd, London, WC1B 3DA; reproduced by permission of the publishers. All rights reserved.*

241 Dragoon's March [see no. 224]

The "Dragoon's March" is in G major. The first strain is an irregular five-bar phrase; the second is a pleasingly symmetrical eight bars, with a slight pause halfway through, dividing it into two equal four-bar subphrases. From The Complete Country Dance Tunes from "Playford's Dancing Master," *edited by Jeremy Barlow. Copyright 1985 by Faber Music Ltd, London, WC1B 3DA; reproduced by permission of the publishers. All rights reserved.*

Phrase Length

Marches, like dances, are largely defined by the way they encourage us to move. As bipeds, we tend to move in patterns built of twos: left, right, left, right. Dancing can be looked at as a kind of stylized walking, and therefore the patterns of music for dancing are often much more intricate than the march, which must always be regular. We use the term meter to describe the regularly recurring emphasis in music, an emphasis that is essential in the dance as well as the march. The meter of the music gives it an underlying pulse, and the phrases are built up of various patterns of these pulses. The phrases of a march or a dance tune are usually built up of symmetrical pairs; two steps times four makes an easily felt pattern of eight steps. Double that again, and with sixteen steps, your group of soldiers is starting to cover some ground. These very regular patterns of eight and sixteen steps are repeated over and over again in the history of fife and drum music. But the dance tunes of the sixteenth and seventeenth centuries were by no means always so regular. Complex combinations of steps led to irregular phrasing, and phrases of eight or sixteen steps could alternate with phrases of, say, twenty.

Dances were often paired in slow-fast combinations, such as the pavane and galliard, and duple and triple divisions of the measure were common; the same melodies were even presented often in both types of meter. I imagine that Queen Elizabeth's fifers and drummers, reportedly present in the household on the evenings when dancing was a very common entertainment, would have known at least some of these more complex ways of expressing the musical pulse that were so important in the musical life of their time.

Elizabethan England to New England

Swiss military music spread across Europe. By 1492 Henry VII of England was paying "two Sweches grete taborers" for their work (*New Grove Dictionary of Music* 1980, 6:540). Both fife and drum are recorded among the instruments providing dinner music for Elizabeth I (regnant 1558–1603). Music was always a prominent feature at the Elizabethan court, for the queen loved music and played both the lute and especially the virginal (a type of harpsichord, so-called because instruction in this instrument was commonly given to young ladies of gentle family). Often court functions were held in a large hall with entertainments going on as the queen talked with her favorites and those close to the power of the kingdom plotted and strategized. Fifers and drummers were among those present at such times. According to a contemporary report, "Elizabeth used to be regaled during dinner with twelve trumpets and two kettle-drums; which, together with fifes, cornets, and side-drums [the military snare drum played on the drummer's left side], made the hall ring for half an hour together" (quoted in Elson 1900, p. 201).

If we do not know much about the exact music the fifers and drummers played, we do have an impression of their effect. Unfortunately, many people get their impressions of this old fife and drum music from our entertainment industry. Contrary to the extremely placid effects (and incompetent playing techniques) illustrated even in some of our best historical films (such as the *Elizabeth* series featuring Helen Mirren and Jeremy Irons, or Olivier's *Henry V*), Shakespeare offers us a glimpse into the uses of the fife and drum that suggests a much more red-blooded, viscerally exciting world.

As Othello, a lifelong military man, sees his world come crumbling down around him, he bids farewell to all that he has held dear and honorable, all that has made the military life worth living. Unlike the traditional reluctant American citizen-soldier's ambivalence toward military service (doing his duty in the hope of returning home to a peaceful hearth—once a familiar American trope, now apparently lost), Othello celebrates the martial life on its own terms:

Farewell the plumed troops, and the big wars
That make ambition virtue! O, farewell!
Farewell the neighing steed and the shrill trump,
The spirit-stirring drum, th' ear-piercing fife,
The royal banner, and all quality,
Pride, pomp, and circumstance, of glorious war!
(Othello, act 3, scene 3)

In our day, when our most impressive engines of war are stealth bombers, remote-controlled missiles, killer drones, and the whole panoply of modern technology, Shakespeare reminds us of a time when war was fought on a more human scale, and delight could be taken in a plumed helmet or a lively drum beating, and a sense of pageantry and display as well as the ruthless excitement and lust for victory that conflates ambition and virtue. Like the plumed helmets and the fine warhorses, the drum and fife were part of that exciting, dangerous, and violent world.

The shrillness of the fife, the rhythmic power of the drum excite not only martial responses but also a more generalized atmosphere of sociability and frivolity. A certain tolerance is granted even today to fifers and drummers who are given to pronounced bouts of festive merriment. The instruments seem to draw out whatever inclination may reside within one for letting propriety slip and replacing it, if only momentarily, with a determination to partake of simple pleasure. This aspect of the instruments' character was present right from the beginning, and Shakespeare uses it to comic effect. In *The Merchant of Venice*, the wealthy moneylender Shylock orders his daughter to close the windows to block out the raucous fifing and drumming that signals dissolute parties and festivities: a masque is a kind of festival with eating, drinking, aspects of theatre and (always) music (not too dissimilar from a drum corps muster today):

What! are there masques? Hear you me, Jessica:
Lock up my doors: and when you hear the drum,

And the vile squeaking of the wry-neck'd fife,
clamber not you up to the casement, then,
Nor thrust your head into the public street,
To gaze on Christian fools with varnish'd faces;
But stop mine house's ears,—I mean, my casements:
Let not the sound of shallow foppery enter
My sober house.

Here Shakespeare emphasizes Shylock's distance from the dominant Christian culture. As a Jewish moneylender, he is far removed from the demotic festivities and the "shallow foppery" of the unlettered, unwashed, and unmoneyed. These two examples from Shakespeare illuminate the double character of the fife and drum: they represent the pageantry, power, and ordered violence of the military but also the festive sociability and intoxicating freedom of the masque.

As Shakespeare here suggests, the uses of the fife and drum in these early days were significantly different from what we think of today as a fife and drum corps: first, the size of the group was always very small: it would have been common to hear a single drummer providing military signals or a marching beat for a group of soldiers, or a single fifer improvising or playing familiar folk melodies. Although massed field music may have been used occasionally, no particular provision seems to have been made for these occasions. Large ensembles seem not to have been organized or rehearsed in any special way, and arrangements requiring additional numbers of players are unheard of: more players meant that more people played, and that was all.

By the later days of Elizabeth's reign, the establishment of English settlements in America was seriously being attempted. Many of us forget that the first and most influential colony in the creation of the United States was named in Elizabeth's honor by her courtier Walter Raleigh. Elizabeth famously remained unmarried, her sovereignty undiluted by marriage to another royal house, and she was widely known by the soubriquet "the virgin queen," hence, Virginia. Thomas Hariot, who wrote the first history of Virginia, dedicated it "to the honneur of yours most soueraine Lady and Queene ELIZABETZ nowe named VIRGINIA."

After Elizabeth died in 1603 and the crown passed to James Stuart I (James VI of Scotland), her elaborately balanced policy of partial religious toleration crumbled. The rigidly doctrinaire Puritan sect in particular was outraged by the resurgence of Catholicism, and some of its members took

The Militia Company of Captain Frans Banning Cocq and of Lieutenant Willem van Ruytenburch, *by Rembrandt van Rijn, is generally considered the greatest painting that includes a field drummer among its subjects. The drum rests on the drummer's left leg, and the characteristic left-hand stick grip enables him to avoid hitting the rim of the drum, which sits at an angle to his body. This painting is contemporary with the early settlements of Connecticut and shows the type of drum and the playing techniques of the period. Probably no one in Connecticut at the time possessed the finery exhibited by these glorious Dutch burghers. Reprinted courtesy of Amsterdam Rijksmuseum*

refuge in the Low Countries. While living in Amsterdam, they may well have observed the town drummer, a civic position immortalized in 1642 by Rembrandt von Rijn in his painting known as *The Night Watch* (formally known as *The Militia Company of Captain Frans Banning Cocq and of Lieutenant Willem van Ruytenburch*). The painting depicts a militia company of Dutch burghers, who commissioned it from the famous local artist.

These were not common soldiers but members of an elite social club performing an honorary function in the city. The drum, like the arquebus and the halberd, is a visual link to the group's military origin. The town drummer would announce public events, attracting crowds to listen to public proclamations; in a time before the widespread use of clocks and watches, he would mark the hours of the day and announce the commencement of public events. Here we see the drummer providing a signal, calling the troops to order (they are clearly not marching in step). The playing technique is recognizably modern: the drum appears to be slung over the right shoulder and resting on the drummer's left leg. The drum rests at an acute angle, necessitating the unique left-hand stick grip that beginners have struggled with for centuries. The drum's construction is virtually the same as those used by Connecticut's fife and drum corps today. Leather ears are used to tension the continuous piece of rope that is threaded through the hoops that hold the drumheads onto the shell. Snares, providing a rattling vibration, are visible on the bottom head of the drum. This painting, contemporary with the earliest English settlements in Connecticut (which had commenced in the 1630s) shows the type of military field drum used in the seventeenth century.

Obtaining a grant from the Stuart monarchy to establish a colony in America (in Virginia, really) the band of Puritans who had moved to the Low Countries returned to England to make their final plans and then set sail in 1620 from the town of Plymouth in Devonshire. Their single ship, the *Mayflower*, included, along with the other necessities of life, a drum: for signaling the church service on Sunday, for calling town meetings, for sounding the alarm in case of fire or attack. The seventeenth-century alternative to sounding the drum was to ring the church bells, but there would be no church bells in New England for many years to come. Bells were heavy and bulky to transport in the small ships that provisioned New England, and foundries were not set up in the New World until a later stage in its economic development.

The Puritans who settled New England were eager to establish a society of pristine virtue, or in a phrase their most famous leader, John Winthrop, borrowed from the Gospel of Matthew, "A City on a Hill," that would be an example of Christian virtue to all humanity. The few hundred Puritan settlers who chose to leave England for the uncharted wilderness of the New World in the 1620s and 1630s believed in a Christianity so strict and austere that all forms of frivolity were banned from their society. In reaction to what they perceived as the licentiousness of English life—the lewdness of the denizens of the cities and the pomp and cupidity of the lords, all given into the spiritual keeping of a salacious and venal clergy—they were determined to make the New World and its Christian society a model for true Christian life. There were to be no ostentatious displays of wealth, whether in architecture, or gardens, or servants, and no celebrations of earthly pleasures: no sumptuous or extravagant clothing, no books of love poetry or madrigals, no dancing, and certainly no frivolous music making. The drum, as a useful tool for signaling across large distances, was an acceptable instrument so long as its use was restricted to its proper duties, but there was little place for the fife in early colonial New England, for the Puritans were not a lighthearted people, and the fife is essentially a comic instrument.

The strictures of these Puritans were too severe to last. At least, they were too severe for the English who came to New England, and for the children who were born to them here in America. Within a couple of generations, the "City on a Hill" had become tainted with jealousy, greed, envy, and all the other qualities human society has never escaped. Alcoholic drinks were served in unbecoming quantity in the ordinary houses (or taverns) that offered respite along the roads connecting the English settlements, and became centers of a more free (or lax) approach to human behavior. By around 1700, the growth of trade and industry (shipbuilding, fishing) had created a new variation on English society in which the Congregational church was the center of town life and determined many of the social norms. The New England towns were relatively free of the overlordship of the hereditary aristocracy and the power of the royal court. Although the Pilgrim Fathers had not succeeded in creating a strict, moralistic theocracy in New England, they had created a way for English people to live that was new, self-consciously distinct, and relatively democratic.

The Sunday church services in Congregational New England were mandatory. (No town could be incorporated without a Congregational church, and no man could vote without church membership. No woman could vote, of course, at all.) Town meetings, which many historians consider to be the signal achievement of colonial New England, were open discussion forums in which all citizens were entitled to have their say. An important civic obligation and social opportunity was afforded by the training days, during which the men of each town were required to train with weapons and attempt to perform military evolutions on the village green to provide for the common defense. These trainbands, or militia groups, were the original model for our National Guard.

In the early days, before bells were hung in church belfries, and when clocks were extremely rare, all of these events were usually regulated by the beating of the drums. A drummer was an important functionary in the town, and a paid employee. For instance, soon after the early Connecticut town of

Wallingford was established in 1670, its town meeting voted that "Jeremiah How, have 40s [shillings] allowed him for beating the drum, Sabbath days and other days." The next year, 20 shillings were allocated by town meeting vote for "beating the drum, Sabbaths, lecture days, trainings, and *keeping in repair*." By 1696, as the town had grown in size, the drummer was ordered to beat the drum throughout the town, with his itinerary ordered "so that the drummer had to go through nearly the whole settled portion of the village." The town records show that this custom was kept up into the second decade of the eighteenth century, when it was (probably) replaced by a church bell (Davis 1870, pp. 415–417).

Firmly ensconced in the towns and among the militia by the late seventeenth century, the drums figure with some prominence in one of the defining moments of Connecticut's history. During the reign of the last Stuart king, James II, a series of attempts were made to revoke or limit Connecticut's charter and turn much of its control over to the crown colony of New York. This series of disputes gave birth to the story of the charter oak. Representatives of the king came to Connecticut to revoke the charter (the founding document of Connecticut) and met with the Connecticut officials in Hartford. According to the legend, one courageous colonist arranged for a blast of wind to blow out the candles that lit the room, abstracted the charter, and hid it in the hollow of a large old oak tree. Unable to seize this essential document, the king's men returned to New York and continued plotting.

Their next major scheme involved an attempt to usurp command of the Connecticut militia. The New Yorkers promised, as politicians always do, that they would not in any way alter the essential rights and privileges of any loyal citizens, but insisted that it was the wish of the king that the Connecticut militia be under the command of the New York government. A Colonel Bayard and a Colonel Fletcher accompanied New York's governor to Hartford to effect what would have amounted to suzerainty over Connecticut. Connecticut's most famous historian, Benjamin Trumbull, tells the story in his 1818 account:

> The trainbands of Hartford assembled, and, as the tradition is, while captain Wadsworth, the senior officer, was walking in front of the companies, and exercising the soldiers, colonel Fletcher ordered his commission and instructions to be read. Captain Wadsworth instantly commanded "Beat the drums"; and there was such a roaring of them that nothing else could be heard. Colonel Fletcher commanded silence, But no sooner had Bay-

> ard made an attempt to read again, than Wadsworth commands, "Drum, drum, I say." The drummers understood their business, and instantly beat up with all the art and life of which they were master. "Silence, silence," says the colonel. No sooner was there a pause, than Wadsworth speaks with great earnestness, "Drum, drum, I say": and turning to his excellency, said, "If I am interrupted again I will make the sun shine through you in a moment." He spoke with such energy in his voice and meaning in his countenance that no further attempts were made to read or enlist men. Such numbers of people collected together, and their spirits appeared so high, that the governor and his suit judged it expedient, soon to leave the town and return to New-York. (Trumbull 1818, 1:393)

These stories illuminate quotidian features of colonial life. The colonists are tied to the concrete: a charter can't be revoked if it can't be physically produced; the command of the militia can't be transferred if the militiamen can't hear the orders read. And the role of the drummers is interesting for what it says not only about the dispute with New York but also about their position within the militia, as well as what it implies about the position of militia drummers when Trumbull wrote his history. These drummers are not cute little drummer boys innocuously tapping out an innocuous beat but men who can beat drums with "all the art and life of which they were master." This story marks the first time, and far from the last, that the Connecticut militia drummers were spoken of respectfully.

Throughout the eighteenth century, the trainbands or militia continued to play an important role in village and town life. As the colonies became more populous and the populations more varied, New England became less an orderly theocracy and more an assemblage of agricultural and merchant communities connected by a series of stage routes, turnpikes, and coastal shipping. As more of the colonists were American born and had never seen England, even the Connecticut place names that were once a comforting reminder of an ancient homeland, such as Coventry, Durham, Torrington, Guilford, lost their associations, becoming merely local references. During the Seven Years' War (1756–1763) between Great Britain and France (known in America as the French and Indian War) the New England militias were engaged, often under British command, to undertake actions against French Canada. It was England's attempt to extract payment from the colonies for the costs of this war that led to the War of Independence, or the (1775–1781) and ultimately the creation of the United States of America.

2

A NEW NATION

FOR NEARLY TWO HUNDRED YEARS, many Americans believed the War of Independence had been the defining moment in our common cultural history. The stories that were told about the revolutionary days and the morals drawn from them shaped an important set of ideas about American society. The fife and drum, in their own small way, formed part of that cultural self-image. I believe in American society today these traditional cultural tropes are largely forgotten, having been replaced for most people by contemporary ideas that address the concerns of our own vastly changed society. To place the fife and drum in their historical context, we need to familiarize ourselves not only with the actual use of the fife and drum during the revolutionary period but also with the cultural values that came to be associated with it.

When a cultural norm is in danger of being lost altogether, an attempt is often made to formalize its fading importance, and in recent years the Connecticut state legislature has done exactly that with what was once our common and informal legacy from the revolutionary period. Within the last thirty-five years, Connecticut has acquired through legislative fiat an official state hero, Nathan Hale, and an official state song, "Yankee Doodle." Understanding something about these two cultural symbols will clarify a good deal about the cultural status of the fife and drum in American mythology.

Nathan Hale, at first blush, would seem an unlikely hero. Born in 1755 into a modestly prosperous farming family in rural Coventry in northeastern Connecticut (whose homestead may still be visited), he attended Yale (at the time, Connecticut's only university) and had just commenced his career as a schoolmaster when the battle of Lexington and Concord irrevocably moved the colonies along the path to armed resistance. Like all able-bodied men, Hale was a member of a militia unit and therefore had already acquired some rudimentary military training. He took a commission in the elite Knowlton's

Nathan Hale. This engraving shows Hale as he is about to be hanged by the British, uttering his famous defiant patriotic statement. Photo courtesy of Sally Rothenhaus

Rangers and by the summer of 1776 was serving with George Washington's army outside New York City. Washington needed to know the state of affairs in the city, and Hale volunteered to serve as one of his spies. When the British captured him as he attempted to return to Washington's army and summarily hanged him, his widely reported (perhaps apocryphal) last words were: "I regret that I have but one life to give for my country." That, in capsule form, is the story of Connecticut's state hero, whose fame in Connecticut was much greater, I believe, before he was raised to this official status. He achieved no dashing exploits in the heat of battle, he had no long and distinguished military record, and his single notable assignment ended in failure. Why, then, is his story remembered and commemorated more than that of, say, Israel Putnam? Putnam, a prosperous and successful businessman, was an outspoken political leader favoring independence in the years leading up to the revolution, served with distinction as part of the elite Rogers' Rangers, was one of Washington's first generals, and commanded troops at the only significant American victory of 1776, the much-commemorated Battle of Bunker Hill. It was Putnam who, according to legend, gave the famous order "Don't fire until you see the whites of their eyes" (perhaps a calumny on the colonists' marksmanship but a great tribute to their nerve).

Hale is honored not because he achieved much but—as has been drummed into generations of Connecticut schoolchildren—because he strove for such worthwhile goals so persistently. The Connecticut legend of

Nathan Hale glorifies respect for high ideals and service to one's community. If traditional British society ordained that respect and privilege were associated with birth and class, the new American society would grant its greatest respect to those who demonstrated civic virtue. When Hale left his family's farm in Coventry for Yale, he showed a healthy thirst for knowledge, for becoming part of a larger world. At Yale, he was not at the top of his class or singled out for extraordinary opportunities. When he left the university he became a schoolmaster. This was not such a lofty achievement for a Yale man of his time, but it enhanced the sense of civic virtue that colors his legend: his decision to teach in the small schoolhouses of New London and East Haddam redounded to the benefit of the citizens of those towns. When Washington called for volunteers, Hale signed up for the extra danger and rigor that Knowlton's elite rangers took on, but there is no evidence that he did any great deeds in their service. But when Washington needed spies, Hale volunteered for that, too, knowing he would be hanged if caught. And of course he was caught, and was hanged. If there is any truth at all to the story of his last words, he never lost sight of the importance of service to his community. In remembering Hale over the centuries, Connecticut honored not a Homeric hero—bold, impetuous, cunning, often victorious, and always concerned with his own glory—but something more homely: a hero on a New England scale who humbly used his imperfect human talents as best he could in service to the good of his community.

The story of "Yankee Doodle," whose origins are less well documented than the life of Nathan Hale, offers another, more rusticated version of republican virtue. When I was a schoolboy, we all sang patriotic songs and folk songs every week in music class, which preserved a familiarity not only with traditional music such as "Yankee Doodle" (we used to sing six verses or so) but even with beautiful folk ballads such as "Barbara Allen" and "Greensleeves."

Yankee Doodle went to town,
Riding on a pony,
Stuck a feather in his hat,
And called it macaroni.

Chorus: Yankee Doodle, Keep it up,
Yankee Doodle Dandy,
Mind the music and the step,
And with the girls be handy.

(A)

(B)

*"Yankee Doodle" as written in the commonplace book of Giles Gibbs, a revolutionary war soldier from Ellington, Connecticut (*A*; this is an earlier version of the tune, and not accurately transcribed) and in a manual by the Civil War colonel H. C. Hart, who was trained in Middletown (*B*). Giles Gibbs manuscript reproduced by permission of the Connecticut Historical Society, Hartford, Connecticut; digitally enhanced facsimile of the Hart manual courtesy of Edmund W. Boyle*

Antiquarians and historians of various types have attempted to trace the origins of the famous song and its doggerel lyrics. When the Connecticut militia were called out in 1745 to invade Canada, two versions of the song were already in existence, and the import of the words was already clear: to British eyes, the colonists were ill-equipped bumpkins, specimens of what Karl Marx later described as "the idiocy of rural life."

The British point of view is not hard to understand. By the mid-eighteenth century, the population of New England largely consisted of people born in America who had never seen a proper city or set foot in a cathedral or even a manor house. The arts and crafts of Europe, from opera to tailoring to gunsmithing to cabinetmaking, were all only vaguely known to the colonists. Even the coarsest British regular would have had some passing familiarity with the finery and elegance of the most privileged European culture, while the farmers and fishers of New England knew only the English Christianity and customs their forefathers had brought with them, and the life they had hewn out of the forest and the sea coast, leavened with whatever small luxuries the ships from Europe brought them.

"Yankee Doodle" was used throughout the War of Independence by the British and in turn by the Americans when, in victory, they mocked the British sense of superiority. As the British marched toward Lexington Green on the morning of April 19, 1775, their fifes and drums reportedly played "Yankee Doodle" to mock the Americans, and as they trailed back to Boston in defeat later the same day, they reported, the Americans played "Yankee Doodle" right back at them.

When Lord Cornwallis surrendered his forces at Yorktown, Virginia, in 1781, in the final battle of the war, "Yankee Doodle" was again in evidence on both sides. A formal surrender of forces in eighteenth-century military life always involved a ceremony, complete with field music and parade. The arms of the defeated were grounded and surrendered to the victors. General Henry Knox, Washington's faithful artillerist since the siege of Boston in 1776, and therefore present at many defeats and humiliations during the course of the war, related gleefully to his wife that the British would not be accorded the pomp and honors they thought their due but would be treated just as they had recently treated the defeated American force at Charleston, South Carolina: "they will have the same honors as the garrison of Charleston; that is, they will not be permitted to unfurl their colors, or play Yankee Doodle." The British protested: Washington did not yield. During the actual ceremony, the British appeared so lackluster that their demeanor implied disrespect to the Americans. French troops, allies with the American cause, were present, and the British apparently felt that it was quite bad enough to surrender to French soldiers, but still worse to Americans, and so the British implied throughout the ceremony that the French were in charge of the surrender, not the (now former) colonists. The Marquis de Lafayette, Washington's favorite and long a trusted assistant in building the

American army, took umbrage and retaliated, in a musical sense. According to an eyewitness:

> It was evident to us that the English in their misfortune were especially mortified to be obliged to lay down their arms before Americans, for the officers and soldiers affected to turn their heads towards the French line. Lafayette perceived this, and revenged himself in a very pleasant manner. He ordered the music of the light infantry to strike up Yankee Doodle. . . . This pleasantry of Lafayette was so bitter to them, that many of them broke their arms in a rage in grounding them on the glacis. (Camus 1976, p. 163)

These stories of Nathan Hale and of "Yankee Doodle" helped to create the image of American society as one in which wealth and worldly sophistication were unimportant. As American schoolchildren were taught for many generations after independence was won, a farmer's son, a local schoolmaster, a failed novice spy could be a hero, and a song lampooning the crudeness of the provincial bumpkin could be taken as a badge of honor. This was to be a society organized for the benefit, as Abraham Lincoln would say in 1863, "of the people, by the people, and for the people." And in a society that glorified the demotic, the humble fife and its companion field drum made an excellent musical accompaniment. For the fife and the drum had been played throughout the famous war when the citizen-soldier had stood up to the professional British regulars, and the fife and drum were the music of the common soldier in daily training, not the ceremonial bands hired by officers for special occasions and to serenade the officer corps and their distinguished guests. No, the fife and drum provided the rough-and-ready music that accompanied the private soldier with a pack on his back, a musket on his shoulder, and a bayonet at his side, prepared to create mayhem in order to drive out the soldiers of an empire he had never asked to join, whose capital he would never see, and whose class system made no sense in the New World. (I am obviously leaving out more sophisticated, or merely sophistic, explanations of the political situation here in order to show the traditional interpretation taught to American schoolchildren for many generations.)

This is the legend of the American Revolution, and gives some explanation of why the fife and drum were seen as quintessential American symbols for many generations afterward. But how did the field music function during the time of the war? What were the real uses of the fife and drum, before they were obscured by the legends of American democracy?

The Fife and Drum as Utensils of Eighteenth-century Warfare

By the middle of the eighteenth century, the principal military forces of Europe (largely following innovations made in Prussia) consisted of standing armies, or permanent professional groups, as opposed to the trainbands of citizens who could be called up in times of emergency. Common soldiers were not held in high regard, and officers, who ordinarily attained their positions by a combination of family influence and financial largesse, were often haphazardly trained while doing their best to dine and dance in a manner befitting the social status of their families. (Jane Austen, the superkeen observer of the minute social stratifications within British society, describes the officer class in *Pride and Prejudice*; William Makepeace Thackeray illumines the enlisted man's plight in *Barry Lyndon*.)

The infantrymen, who were treated as interchangeable ciphers, often came from the poorest farming families or the least privileged population of the towns and cities. The usual military enticements were invoked to recruit these men, as is shown in William Hogarth's engraving the *March to Finchley*: the regalia of the dress uniform, the rhythmic power of the military drum, the possibility of travel and adventure and of course the king's shilling, all beckoned the indigent into the ranks. When these blandishments failed, impressment, or arbitrary forced enlistment, was practiced. The "press gang," a feared and often loathed institution, was a gang of soldiers or sailors who intimidated and sometimes cudgeled the unfortunate into years of military servitude.

In this turbulent and dangerous military world, the music was divided in the same way as the men themselves. For the officers and for high military functions there was often a regimental band, whose instruments included clarinets, oboes, and horns, with kettledrums added when possible. These bands were often paid out of the officers' private incomes and performed mostly on ceremonial occasions and for the officer corps. The field music, on the other hand, employed trumpets (resembling a bugle more than a modern-day valved trumpet) for the cavalry and fifes and drums for the foot soldiers. In the British army the exact number of fifers and drummers was rarely specified, but one or two drummers were assigned to each company. The drums themselves had become much smaller. The twenty- or even twenty-two-inch drumheads of the seventeenth century were replaced for the most part by ones as small as fifteen or sixteen inches. For ceremonial occasions, the fifers and drummers of each regiment or brigade were massed

March to Finchley, *by William Hogarth. This famous engraving shows the finery of the dress regalia of the troops, as well as the use of the fife and drum. Reprinted courtesy of Yale Center for British Art, Paul Mellon Collection*

and performed as a single unit. A drum major and a fife major were assigned to each regiment; their job was to ensure that the music was correctly played whenever required, so they were in charge of the discipline as well as teaching of the fifers and drummers.

The music these fifers and drummers officially played falls into two categories: signals (also known as "calls" or "duties") and marches. The signals were a way of notifying the soldiers of the necessary activities in the camp and on the field: calls included the reveille, the retreat, a call for adjutants and one for sergeants, a pioneer's call announcing that soldiers would be leaving camp to forage for food and firewood, the rogue's march announcing a punishment detail, and so forth. Every day when the army was encamped, there would be a full mustering of the troops. Orders

Southwark Fair, *by William Hogarth. The drum, here played by a woman, is associated with the informal excitement of street entertainment in eighteenth-century England. Reprinted courtesy of Yale Center for British Art, Paul Mellon Collection*

would be read, deserters would be discovered, and a general assessment of the state of the troops could be undertaken. A frequent ceremony was the trooping of the colors, in which the identifying flags of each regiment were paraded in front of the men. In an age of very limited literacy, this practice enabled soldiers to learn to identify their unit by its identifying insignia—its battle flag. The fifes and drums were an integral part of all such ceremonies.

The evening ceremonies that ended the day's activities were signaled by the retreat call, which was followed later in the evening by the tattoo. Not only employed in military encampments, these ceremonies and signals were part of the daily life of Europeans, and citizens who were not engaged in the military knew them well. When the philosopher Jean-Jacques Rousseau was a teenager and eager to escape the drudgery of his apprenticeship in Geneva, he tried to stay out of the city on Sundays for as long as he could, but he knew that when the retreat sounded, the gates of the city would close soon afterward. In his *Confessions* he writes: "About half a league from the city I heard the retreat sounded: I doubled my pace; I heard the tattoo beat, and ran with all my might. I arrived out of breath and bathed in perspiration; my heart beat, from a distance I saw the soldiers at their posts. . . . Twenty paces from the outposts, I saw the first bridge raised" (p. 38).

The second group of pieces, those for marching, have raised a number of probably insoluble problems for everyone since the eighteenth century who has tried to understand the subject: the characteristics of the types of marching step used and the distinctions between them. Most of the training and marching of soldiers in formation took place at a very slow pace, or common time, as it was called: in the British army, the common time was beat at sixty beats per minute, or one step per second. If you try this pace, you will see that it requires an exaggeratedly slow step. The Prussia-trained Baron Friedrich von Steuben, who drilled Washington's troops beginning in 1778, chose to change the common time to about seventy-five steps per minute, and this became the common time of the Washington's Continental Army. Try this step and you will see that it is an easier, more comfortable stride, though still slower than most people's normal walk. Another cadence used in training was the quickstep. Both von Steuben's manual and the British regulations of the day stipulate a step of about 120 beats per minute for the quick step, just double the tempo of the common time. (John Moon, distinguished historian of martial music and formerly drum major of Her Majesty's Brigade of Guards at Buckingham Palace, teaches that the British military step has traditionally been regulated by simple ratios from the sixty-step-per-minute common time. Thus, 60, 90, or 120 steps per minute are all tempi appropriate for marchers within this tradition.) The quickstep was used for maneuvering on the field. It is obviously an advantage if troops can deploy rapidly into formation, and the quickstep, learned with extensive training, was an important tactic in infantry maneuvering. Elite troops such as grenadiers often marched at the quickstep on all occasions, emphasizing the razor sharpness of their training. (The idea of elite troops marching extra fast continued for a long time. My father, who was in basic training at Fort Bragg in 1941, told me that the Army Rangers marched everywhere at the double time. My father also said that all the Rangers were crazy, and he would know.)

The tune "Roslin Castle" can be played as a common time march, and is associated with funeral services. Digitally enhanced facsimile courtesy of Edmund W. Boyle

In addition, during the trooping of the colors an especially slow step was used: the "troop," or "singlings of the troop." For this step, a whole genre of pieces were created in 3/8 time; the soldiers took one step per measure, about forty to fifty steps per minute. These steps are closely related to the triple-meter dances of the eighteenth century, such as the minuet and the German Ländler, which developed into the waltz during the late Napoleonic era.

Several transcriptions of common time marches (often called grand marches) survive from eighteenth-century sources (including excerpts from the works of so great a composer as Mozart). In character the best of them tend toward the pompous, while the rest hover dangerously close to the merely tedious. A few, such as the "Bedfordshire March," and the funereal "Roslin Castle," achieve the stateliness and measured formality of tone that was much valued in eighteenth-century society.

But that the majority of these marches are mediocre at best seems to me an inescapable assessment, even though many seventeenth- and eighteenth-century composers wrote many marches, and they are often quite grand. But the fife, alas, is not the ideal instrument for realizing them. With its limited range, and the inability of any but the very, very best fifers to play in tune in more than a couple of keys, the more musically intricate marches are beyond the limits of military field music. Remember that the fife had remained unchanged for centuries, while the eighteenth-century composers were accustomed to writing for instruments with more refined capabilities. Pieces that modulate through several keys, bass lines that need to be strongly brought out, harmonies that need to be precisely in tune are not the stock-in-trade of the field musician.

So the marches we find in the eighteenth-century fife manuscripts and instruction books are relatively straightforward. The transcriptions of drum beatings that we have from this period are also quite simple and employ only a handful of rudiments, mostly limited to rolls of various lengths, the flam, the ruff, the drags, and some slow paradiddles. However, the purpose of these common time marches was to provide a strong marching beat for troops, not ornate concert music. And whatever their weaknesses as concert music, when well played and particularly when experienced as part of a formal ceremony, many of the grand marches can live up to the name and produce an effect of quite remarkable formality and grandeur.

The quickstep is another matter entirely. The tunes played for the quicksteps are usually in 2/4 or 6/8 meter. Many of the quickstep tunes that have come down to us are dances: jigs, reels, cotillions, and so forth. The few quickstep drum beatings that we have are also quite simple, although fitting in the drum rolls cleanly at this tempo is quite challenging. The quickstep was used less frequently than the common time in military training (though of great importance in its place). Many of the quicksteps are lively and are obviously related to some of the more vigorous dances of the day. Fifers seemed to prefer them; many of the fife music manuscripts from the period show many more quicksteps than common time marches.

The distinction between the two types of marching step and the pieces appropriate for each is not absolute. Even the Prussian von Steuben writes that the common time step should be "about" seventy-five steps per minute. But how could one tell exactly? The metronome with its pendulum ticktock was not in regular use until the early 1800s. Using pocket watches to measure steps and time was hardly possible; watches were expensive and fragile. Yet daily repetition, when accompanied with good concentration, can allow people to learn all sorts of musical detail. I have no doubt at all that there were sergeants in all the eighteenth-century armies who trained their troops to march to their desired cadence within a tolerance of fewer than five beats per minute. I also believe that in the local militias, practicing a couple of times a year on the town green, perhaps with a good drummer or perhaps with one who didn't know his rudiments and beatings at all, there must have been many chaotic examples of ragtag marching, and when these militias joined together in regimental strength, the unhappy results, gleefully mocked by the British in reports, letters, and "Yankee Doodle," are easily understood. This lack of uniform training exacted a severe toll (in lives lost, victories forestalled, morale broken) on Washington's army in the early years of the war. The local militias were supposed to provide training, but it was often inadequate; and the training of those who enlisted in the army was often very poor. By the time the soldiers were on campaign, they should have been trained but often weren't. Any soldier thus deprived would pay the price for his incompetence.

Nonetheless, the completely inflexible application of rules from a book is hardly typical of the eighteenth century, when bureaucratic efficiency was not even an understood concept, much less a way of life. Differences in training, in experience, in the temperament of the officer corps would surely have influenced the details of the drill used in various encampments. The tendency was to moderate the extremes of tempo. When von Steuben introduced his more rapid common time step at Valley Forge, one of the American soldiers wrote: "This forenoon the Brigade went thro the Manouvers under the direction of Baron Stuben the step is about half way betwixt Slow and Quick time an easy and natural step and I think much better than the former" (Ewing 1928, p. 34; quoted in Camus). When General Washington held a grand parade as the troops marched through Philadelphia in August 1777, he ordered that the fifers and drummers be grouped by brigade, creating very large ensembles, 80 to 120 musicians per brigade by one expert's estimate (Camus 1976, p. 89), and ordered them to play at the quickstep, "but with such moderation, that the men may step to it with ease; and without dancing along, or totally disregarding the music, as too often has been the case" (Fitzpatrick 1931–1944, 9:127; quoted in Camus).

After forty-five years of playing American fife and drum music and teaching others to march and to play, I read Washington's order with great satisfaction. A cadence of 120 steps to the minute is just too fast a tempo for any but the most elite ensembles to march comfortably while playing these quicksteps. And, given the heavy weapons, packs, and accoutrements of the eighteenth-century soldier, this quickstep tempo is quite impractical for soldiers marching any significant distance. When slowed down to just about 110 beats per minute, though, one can walk for miles, comfortably in time, and with good precision. It seems that Washington may have felt the same. The "true" quickstep of 120 beats per minute was surely a useful stratagem for deploying troops on the field, but for covering long distances, it was perhaps asking too much.

The fife and drum during the American War for Independence were not, of course, exclusively played under strict military control under the orders of Washington and according to the prescriptive rules of von Steuben. The much-maligned local militias, it is true, were no match for the British regulars, and Washington was persistently frustrated in his efforts to control or even predict their movements. But these were the groups of ordinary citizens who were willing to leave their homes and families for limited periods and face the British army and its hired mercenaries in battle. This seems no small thing. The amateurishness of the troops was no doubt reflected in a field music that was not all one might have wished, and Washington obviously had too many important issues to deal with in training and maneuvering his army to worry overmuch about the state of his field music. Some small inkling of the kinds of dilemmas he constantly faced in trying to create an army that would stand up to the British is shown in different orders he issued at different times regarding this small detail of his duties. Recognizing the morale-building qualities of music for his men, he issued a famous order:

> The music of the Army being in general very bad; it is expected, that the drum and fife Majors exert themselves to improve it, or they will be reduced, and their extraordinary pay taken from them. Stated hours to be assigned, for all the drums and fifes, of each regiment, to attend them and practice—Nothing is more agreeable, and ornamental, than good music; every officer, for the credit of his corps, should take care to provide it. (Fitzpatrick 1931–1944, 8:181–182)

The fife and drum majors Washington refers to here were the chief musicians in each regiment, charged, as his order implies, with the order and teaching of the field musicians. Documentary evidence suggests that not all officers shared Washington's enthusiasm for good-quality field music, or perhaps they did not think it difficult to procure. By the end of the war, musicians who had been enlisted as fifers and drummers were considered supererogatory, and field musicians were to be selected from the ranks. According to a general order of 1782:

> Resolved, that in future no recruit shall be inlisted to serve as a drummer or fifer. When such are wanted, they shall be taken from the soldiers of

> the corps in such numbers and of such description as the Commander in Chief or commanding officer of a separate army shall direct, and be returned back and others drawn out as often as the good of the service shall make necessary. (Camus 1976, p. 168)

From among this motley crew of fifers, drummers, and those merely ordered to become one or the other, there must have emerged quite a variety of musical (or perhaps protomusical) sounds. Surely, these were difficult times, and much of the field music, as Washington himself commented, was clearly inadequate. But the picture is more complex than these often-quoted statements make it appear. For instance, who were those adult fifers and drummers who signed on to the army as field musicians? Presumably the majority of them must have been militia fifers and drummers—descendants, in Connecticut's case, of those who drowned out the orders of the king's men back in the 1680s.

I find it implausible to think that a musical tradition already stretching to the earliest colonial settlements should have failed to produce some competent practitioners. But of the exact drum beatings they played we know almost nothing. A few beginner exercises, a few drum beatings that may well go back to the late eighteenth century, are all we have. This is not surprising to me. There was no standard form of notation for drumming in the eighteenth century. Various kinds of shorthand systems indicate successions of rudiments in a musical phrase, but without the assistance of an experienced drummer of the time who understood the shorthand, there is no way to learn the correct execution of the old drum beatings. As far back as we can trace it, field drumming in Connecticut (and not only there) remained an oral art, passed down from generation to generation through personal contact and demonstration. While we know some details of the eighteenth-century drumming style, we cannot know how well it was executed, or how wide a variety of drum beatings the most accomplished drummers used. I believe that some of them must have been quite expert drummers, and must have had their little secrets, the intricate beatings of the elite drummers of the day. I have never encountered a culture of drummers that didn't have such an elite as part of its tradition.

Such an idea is supported by what we know of the fifing tradition, in which musical notation does supply a clue to the level of playing. Chance and good fortune have bequeathed to us a surprising number of manuscript books written by eighteenth-century fifers, some accurately notated, others

"Ladies Hope Reele," from the Giles Gibbs manuscript, is an example of a fairly difficult eighteenth-century fife tune. Giles Gibbs manuscript reproduced by permission of The Connecticut Historical Society, Hartford, Connecticut

mere sketches. From them we learn that dozens of tunes were played, some quite difficult and clearly beyond the level of skill that could be expected of soldiers drawn almost at random from the ranks. Giles Gibbs, of Ellington (which borders on Nathan Hale's hometown of Coventry), left a remarkable commonplace book inscribed with marches, quicksteps, and troops, all written in the common fife keys of one or two sharps, and mostly fitting comfortably in the range of the instrument. The Thomas Remington manuscript (from Rhode Island) contains fewer tunes, but includes a very nice version of the famous "College Hornpipe," one that presents an interesting problem.

As written, this version of "College Hornpipe" goes beyond the normal range of the instrument, making it extremely difficult to play. By considering the difficulties presented in this piece, I hope the reader will gain some insight into the nature of the fife, and of fifing. While the B in the fife's third octave (B3) is considered the top of the fife's range, this hornpipe continues up to the D above this (D4), a note which most fifes emit only with great difficulty, more a shriek than a definite pitch.

Was this Remington's intention? Or did he merely copy down a favorite tune, perhaps with the assistance of a violinist, for whom the range would

Version of the well-known "College Hornpipe" written down in Rhode Island during the American Revolution. Reproduced by permission of John Hay Library, Brown University

not be a problem, and only later realize that the piece was extremely difficult? Or did he play the piece an octave lower?

I don't think it was Remington's intention to write everything an octave above traditional fife pitch, because this would make nonsense of all the other pieces in the manuscript, which all fit into a comfortable range. The thin bore of the fife, which makes the upper register easier to play, produces a surprisingly thin and weak tone in its first octave. If the tune were played this low, a drum would completely drown out the melody. In addition, the rapid runs in the bottom octave are very difficult to articulate. The obvious solution would have been to transpose the piece to G major, but this

Remington did not do. We'll never know definitively what he intended, but having spent most of my life around New England fifers, I will suggest some possibilities: first, he might not have been musically adept enough to work out comfortably the transposition to the key of G. I have known many fifers who could transpose by ear but just didn't want to take the time to write down the piece again in the new key. If he learned it from a violinist in the key of D (as we have it), he could just have written it down and then realized that this was an extremely awkward piece to play.

Second, quite possibly, he might have been a very good fifer. Playing this extremely lively hornpipe in D would produce an extremely brilliant effect in the upper register, although intonation would surely suffer. Playing it an octave lower, while technically difficult at speed, would produce a very gentle, flute-like sound, ideal for entertaining friends over drink in a tavern. Nearly all the good fifers I have known have valued the dash and brilliance of the upper register, and simply accepted that poor intonation was an inevitable weakness of the instrument. And obstreperous barkeeps and pugnacious tipplers have long established the prudence of playing in the lower range of the fife when indoors. We'll never know for sure what Remington intended, but for any fifer the alternatives his manuscript of "College Hornpipe" presents are worth thinking about.

The fife and drum were an integral part of colonial life. Every militia company was assigned its fifer and drummer, and the fife manuscripts that are still extant give clear evidence that fifers in some communities could give polished performances of a pleasing variety of dance tunes and military music. It is not at all certain that the standard of playing was higher in Washington's Continental Army than among the amateur players. In the army, a soldier who had the potential for leadership or even one who showed potential for the bayonet could be removed from field music duty and put to more germane military tasks. The enforced rehearsal times of the encampments, and the repeated admonitions for improved field music do not convince me that the goal of a polished and effective field music was always met.

When the war was over, at any rate, the remembrance of the field music remained as part of the nascent American legend. As the stories of Nathan Hale and "Yankee Doodle" show, in the American imagination it was not the polished, the precise, or even the victorious that were most valued, but the efforts of ordinary people to strive for something of value, to create an independent and more equitable society. Nathan Hale was hanged as a spy at the age of twenty-one, before completing his very first mission. The

American soldiers were mostly Yankee Doodles, provincial, ill-equipped, and seldom able to win head-to-head battles with British regulars. And the American field music was no doubt something of a motley mismatch of skilled instrumentalists and untalented beginners. But in the burgeoning national consciousness they were all remembered gratefully as the group of individuals who banded together to attempt the realization of the ideals embodied in Mr. Jefferson's Declaration, that "all men are created equal, that they are endowed by their creator with certain unalienable rights, that among these are Life, Liberty, and the pursuit of Happiness."

THE EARLY NATIONAL PERIOD AND THE CIVIL WAR

FOLLOWING THE ESTABLISHMENT of independence, the citizens of the thirteen states had to establish a correct relationship between state and federal powers. It was during this period that Connecticut became more of a manufacturing center, as population began to move toward the factory towns. Some of our nation's earliest industrial achievements were those of Seth Thomas, for whom Thomaston was named, and whose factories created affordable and accurate clocks (as well as metronomes for musicians) and shipped them all around the new country. From there this trade spread to Waterbury, the much larger town nearby. (In *The Picture of Dorian Gray* [1890], Oscar Wilde equips one of his aristocratic English characters with a "Waterbury watch.") Willimantic, the "Thread City," began building its large textile mills, which would employ thousands of workers. The Hitchcock Chair Company, in Riverton in northwestern Connecticut, began its business in 1818. Its popular and sturdy furniture, usually with painted and stenciled decorations, became a distinctive presence in national culture. In my own hometown of East Hampton, the "Bell Town," the first bell manufactory was established in the first decade of the nineteenth century; it rapidly spawned several imitators and related businesses. Bells from East Hampton were shipped all over the country, and the bell factories—Bevin Brothers, Gong Bell, Barton's—were still in business when I was growing up there in the 1950s and 1960s. During the nineteenth century, the great number of small family farms that typified Connecticut in the colonial era were gradually supplanted by factory towns in which small-scale agriculture often provided merely a supplemental income to factory work.

Much of this increase in manufacturing was related to the new ease of communication and commerce created by a unified national government after the ratification of the U.S. Constitution in 1788. However, the individual states retained much more independence than we can easily imagine from our twenty-first-century vantage point. Among the important duties and privileges of each state was the maintenance of an extensive state militia. In southern New England the prospect of attack by either Native American groups or European invaders was slight, but still palpable. The depredations of King Philip's War, in which Connecticut troops had participated, were firmly preserved in local memory. The forests only slightly west of Connecticut's borders gave cover to numerous bands of outlaws and what seemed the mysterious movements of the Native American tribes. When Thomas Jefferson commissioned the Lewis and Clark expedition to explore the continent all the way to the Pacific coast and bought the gigantic Louisiana Purchase (which included the whole of the Mississippi basin from Canada to New Orleans), the need of a military presence to police and help organize these lands was patent. In addition, the British presence in Canada and France's continued interest in North America meant that the possibility of renewed entanglements with old Europe were not to be easily avoided. The United States of America, a fledgling nation governed by an untested and radical system of representative republicanism, was by no means a secure and respected participant in the comity of nations. Indeed, many of the Americans who lived through the revolution were still alive to see the British invade once more at Lake Champlain and burn the newly created capital city of Washington.

It was in the context of these tumultuous and unpredictable events that the United States established its political and cultural institutions, and the state militias in those early years featured prominently as institutions necessary for the common weal. During his first term as president, Washington called for the standardization of the militias so as to have a well-trained and cohesive military force in case of necessity. Participation in the militia was a nearly universal obligation (exceptions were mostly granted to those in necessary administrative occupations), so the whole population would have been familiar with the militia and its traditions and ceremonies. Every company (of sixty-four men) was to have "one drummer, and one fifer or bugler." Ten companies (two battalions) made up a regiment. And each regiment had a fife major and drum major who were given extra pay and whose task it was to train the company fifers and drummers within their regiment. In this way, the fife and drum continued to be a familiar part of life in the new nation. On all muster days, when the various militia units met to train, the fifers and drummers provided (perhaps truncated) versions of the entire military duty that was required of the regular army field music. By the 1820s, more than twenty regiments were listed in the Connecticut State Register. At full regimental strength (admittedly unlikely) a couple of hundred fifers and an equal number of drummers would be militia musicians each year.

The honor of being listed in this annual register (published throughout this early national period by Samuel Green of New London) must have been a motivating factor among the fifers and drummers in the state. During most of these years, Green remembered to include the regimental fife majors and drum majors in his listing of each regiment's officer corps. Looking through the records, I was surprised to see the rapid turnover of these positions: few if any of the fife or drum majors kept their positions for more than two years. This could mean all sorts of contradictory things, but until adequate research is undertaken, speculation is idle. The key fact that the State Register tells us is that there were fifers and drummers all around the state participating in public life, as drummers had in Connecticut since the seventeenth century.

Some of the instruments that were played in this period are still extant. Music shops offering a variety of instruments and often instructional publications as well became common throughout the first half of the nineteenth century. Perhaps the first such shop in New England was that of William Callender of Boston, who made and sold both fifes and drums and also offered band and stringed instruments beginning in the 1790s. Some of his instruments made their way to Connecticut and have survived.

The most famous instruments of this period are the drums made by the Brown family of Bloomfield, Connecticut. Coopering, or barrel-making, had been a family trade, so the wood-bending and joinery skills necessary for drum making were already developed within the family. The most famous Brown was Eli, whose drums seem to have been made from the 1820s to the 1840s. The drums are generally made of one thin piece of maple, sometimes beautifully figured, with the overlapping seam of bent wood glued and fastened with brass tacks. More tacks were often added to the shell in decorative patterns of lines or circles, an old drum maker's tradition. The Browns made both snare and bass drums, but far fewer bass drums survive.

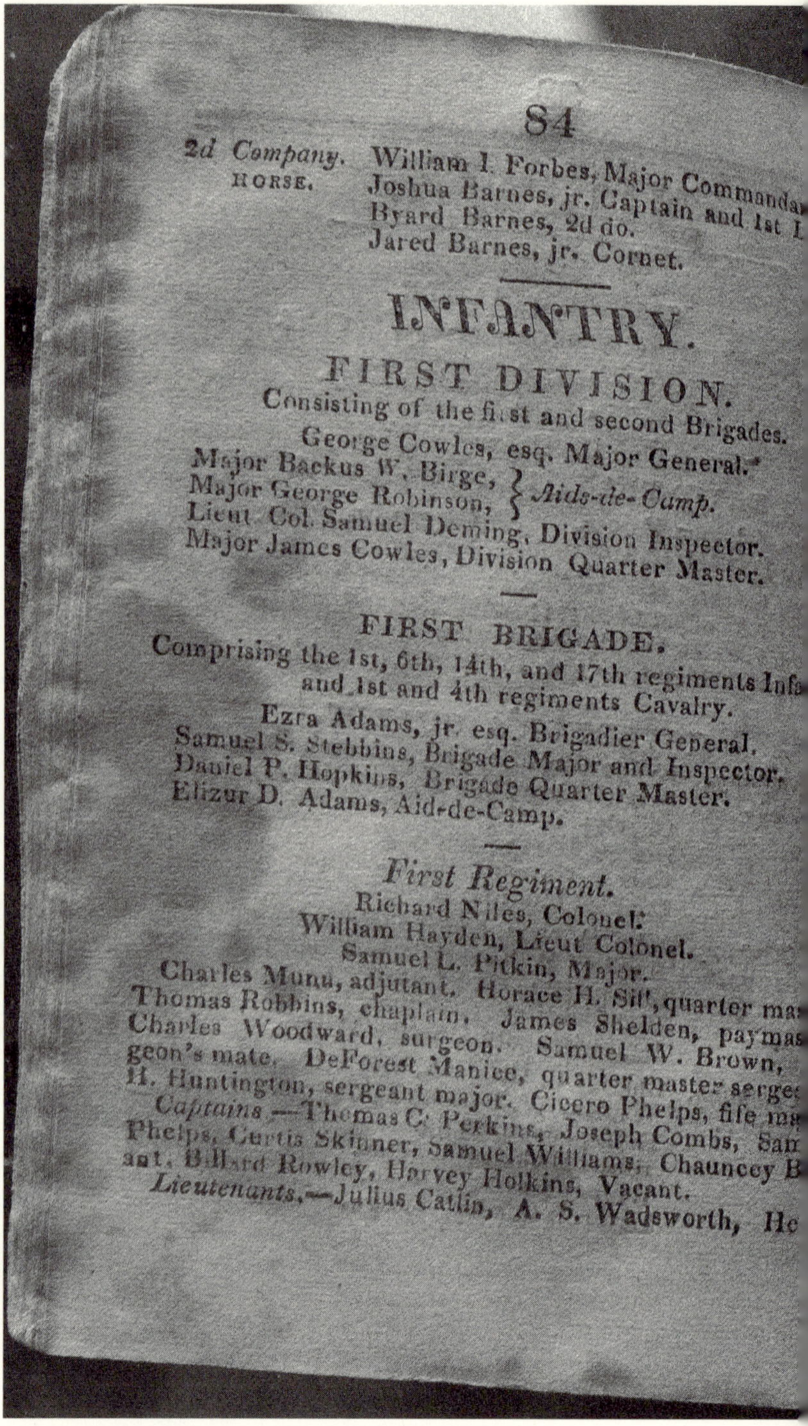
84

2d Company. William I. Forbes, Major Commanda
HORSE. Joshua Barnes, jr. Captain and 1st L
Byard Barnes, 2d do.
Jared Barnes, jr. Cornet.

INFANTRY.

FIRST DIVISION.
Consisting of the first and second Brigades.
George Cowles, esq. Major General.
Major Backus W. Birge, } *Aids-de-Camp.*
Major George Robinson,
Lieut. Col. Samuel Deming, Division Inspector.
Major James Cowles, Division Quarter Master.

FIRST BRIGADE.
Comprising the 1st, 6th, 14th, and 17th regiments Infa
and 1st and 4th regiments Cavalry.
Ezra Adams, jr. esq. Brigadier General.
Samuel S. Stebbins, Brigade Major and Inspector.
Daniel P. Hopkins, Brigade Quarter Master.
Elizur D. Adams, Aid-de-Camp.

First Regiment.
Richard Niles, Colonel.
William Hayden, Lieut. Colonel.
Samuel L. Pitkin, Major.
Charles Munn, adjutant. Horace H. Sill, quarter ma
Thomas Robbins, chaplain. James Shelden, paymas
Charles Woodward, surgeon. Samuel W. Brown,
geon's mate. DeForest Manice, quarter master serge
H. Huntington, sergeant major. Cicero Phelps, fife ma
Captains.—Thomas C. Perkins, Joseph Combs, Sam
Phelps, Curtis Skinner, Samuel Williams, Chauncey B
ant, Billard Rowley, Harvey Holkins, Vacant.
Lieutenants,—Julius Catlin, A. S. Wadsworth, Ho

The Connecticut State Register for the year 1819 lists the regimental fife major and drum major as part of the officer corps. The fife and drum majors were responsible for the training and discipline of the field musicians in their regiment. Photo courtesy of Sally Rothenhaus

aylord, B. O. King, Elisha Risley, Eli Pitkin, Hiram
s, J. B. Chapman, Dryden Holcomb.
gns.—Norman Lyman. A. S. Stillman, James Loo-
, Francis Stoughton, Charles Forbes, Russel Eldridge,
as I. *Hubbard*, Charles Clark, Marcus Griswold.

Flank Companies.

tains.—Alva Blodget, Charles Barnard.
tenants.—Daniel Stocking, Nathaniel Woodhouse.
gns.—Hiram Strong, William Seymore.

Rifle Companies.

tains.—Levi Wells, Thomas Roberts, Elisha An-

tenants.—Lemuel Crane, Elisha Harrington, Grove
er.
igns.—Eli Gillet, §Vacant, Joseph House.

Sixth Regiment.

Joseph Camp, Colonel.
Ozias Camp, Lieut Colonel.
John C. Pratt, Major.

ester Pulsiver, jr. adjutant. P. H. Sellew, quarter
r. Wm. H. Fisk, paymaster. Edward S. Cone, sur-
. Giles M. Boardman, surgeon's mate. Ralph R.
ns, sergeant major. Sidney Smith, quarter master
nt. Samuel G. Wilcox, drum major. Samuel Car-
e major.

ptains.—Elijah Keach, John O. Hayden, Jared Wells,
am Butler, William Bowers. J. Johnson, Sylvester
, J. Dickinson, Levi Coe, Hiram Hodge.
utenants.—L. B. Churchill, William Woodward, Geo.
Thomas Danforth, Linus Wilcox, Spicer Leonard,
ncey Goodale, Vacant, Alfred Bailey, Jesse Loveland.
signs.—Charles Francis 2d, Israel Bailey, Gideon
s, W. W. Bulkley, Bethuel Roberts, Bulkley Wet.
, William White, Lysis Lamb, Wm. P. Stow, H. W.
n.

Flank Company.

ptain.—Josiah Goodrich.
eutenant.—Josiah W. Griswold.
sign.—Ralph Welles.

These drums are typical of those used for training the Connecticut militia in the early nineteenth century. Left: *drum made by Eli Brown, the most famous and finest Connecticut drum maker of the nineteenth century.* Right: *drum made by William Callender of Boston, probably in the late eighteenth century. Callender drum from author's collection; Brown drum courtesy of Museum of Fife and Drum, Ivoryton, Connecticut; photo by Sally Rothenhaus*

These instruments themselves suggest much about the sound as well as the playing techniques of the music they were used for. Most of the Brown drums are large, with heads ranging from about seventeen to nineteen inches. (By comparison, today the head of a typical concert snare drum measures fourteen inches and that of a marching snare drum fourteen or even thirteen inches.) The sticks used on these large militia drums were necessarily long and heavy. In fact, they are the largest snare drum sticks I have ever seen used for any purpose. An eighteen-inch drumhead (particularly one made of calfskin rather than our contemporary plastic or Kevlar) requires a bigger stick to create enough vibration to develop the full tone of the drum, or as we say, to "fill the drum." A modern concert or drum-set stick is about sixteen inches long; a marching percussion stick is

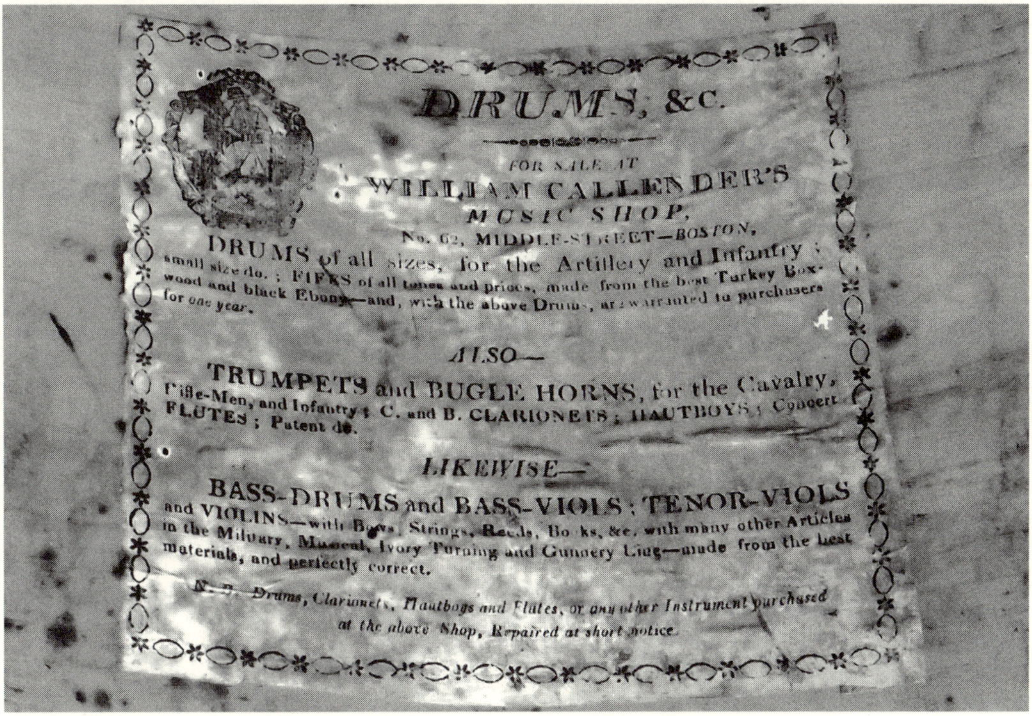

This drum label lists the offerings available in William Callender's Boston shop. The maker's labels were traditionally glued inside the drum shell. Photo by Sally Rothenhaus

seventeen inches or a little shorter. The old Connecticut sticks for "open" drumming are regularly eighteen or eighteen and a half inches and generally made of very heavy woods such as rosewood or ebony. Big sticks used on a big drum create a pretty loud tone and one that also sustains well. This was drumming that was ideally suited for the military signaling that was its primary function. When drilling in battalion strength, five drummers were supposed to set the marching tempo for more than 250 soldiers. Such is these lively drums' rattle and buzz, often heard today when Connecticut's famous Moodus Drum and Fife Corps plays, that a listener has to be about a hundred feet away before an ensemble of this size becomes merely tolerable rather than a din. This was an instrument beautifully designed for its purpose.

The appropriate playing technique to accomplish these instruments' mission probably arose during the early decades of the republic to meet the requirements of militia drumming. Playing the slow common time marches on these large and resonant drums, the drummers practiced a very deliberate and efficient motion, using the whole arm to bring each heavy stick up in preparation for each rudiment. By using the weight of the arm to create power, the drummer could stay quite relaxed while playing loudly for extended periods of time. The style is physically smooth, not forced, and if you see someone bludgeoning a drum, you are not seeing the old open Connecticut style. It is drumming as performed by laborers, or the class we used to describe as "workingmen." As a child, I used to love watching my father handle an axe or a sledgehammer when he was cutting and splitting firewood, and the principles of his motion were very similar to those of the open style of drumming. You use the largest muscles available to you, in your back and your upper arms, to lift the axe up over your head, and then you let gravity bring it down, with a little "snap" of the wrist if you need extra power. My dad could split wood in this way for hours, never seeming to exert too much energy but constantly chopping through thick tree limbs efficiently and smoothly. The old drummers played in much the same manner, always moving smoothly, in constant motion, drumming and marching mile after mile.

During this period sustained efforts to notate military drumming appear for the first time. The late eighteenth century saw great advances in the production of inexpensive books of all sorts. While books (and music) published before this time were often very beautifully produced, they were also very expensive and hence rare. The London of the mid- to late eighteenth century saw the development of "Grub Street" or cheap publications. As Samuel Johnson, greatest of the Grub Street hacks, explained the new trade in his Dictionary, Grub Street was "originally the name of a street in Moorfields in London, much inhabited by writers of small histories, dictionaries, and temporary poems; whence any mean production is called grub street." The early fife and drum manuals strike me as being Grub Street publications, for they are "mean productions," inelegant, inexpensive books for working people rather than elaborate publications designed for a squire's library. Among the problems these manuals' authors and publishers faced was the lack of any system for writing down drum beatings. None of the early attempts is really successful, and there are aspects of these old notations of drum beatings that we may never be able to decipher. In the United States in 1812, Charles Ashworth presented his public with one of the earliest attempts at a practical drum notation (several other musicians, both here and in England, were working on other approaches to the problem at the same time). While the difficulty of writing down the rhythms of a snare drum part appears in no way insuperable to a modern musician, two hundred years ago it was uncharted territory.

Two explanations for the early authors' difficulty in creating a notation system appear to me most plausible. First, many drummers were, I expect, simply drummers, not schooled musicians, and did not read standard musical notation. Second, and more interesting, the standard notation in use at this time was very efficient at conveying basic rhythmic patterns, but when the rhythmic structure became intricate, or ambiguous, a series of approximations and symbols were invented in an attempt to indicate the nuances essential to the more rhythmically subtle musical expression. The eighteenth-century French harpsichordists contrived the most famous examples—a bewildering array of signs for various rhythmic inflections and nuanced embellishments. To listen to a historically informed performance of the *pieces de clavecin* by Francois Couperin "Le Grand" (1668–1733), for instance, is to enter a very rarefied world of rhythmic and agogic nuance. And to look at the score of one of these pieces is to confront a motley of signs whose interpretation requires long study.

In its own admittedly less sophisticated way, military drumming is also difficult to notate. Its musical basis is the ornamentation of basic rhythms. The rolls, flams, ruffs, drags, and various degrees of accent that are essential to the style cannot be shown using the conventions of eighteenth-century rhythmic notation. Just as the harpsichord teachers and composers indicated a general idea with their symbols of ornamentation but assumed that the student would learn primarily by example from the teacher, I believe that the better teachers of drumming in those days thought of rudimental drumming as an art that could only be taught by example and imitation, and therefore devoted very little effort to devising a notational system. If my explanation seems fanciful, note that one of the first effective systems of notation, that of Samuel Potter in his wonderfully named Grub Street treatise *The Art of Beating the Drum* (1817), speaks of the drummer's rudiments in terms exactly like those of the classical musician (even if his definitions are a little provincial): "For a length of time I have been studying in what manner to write the Duty of the side Drum by Note, as that part of Drum beating is so very intricate. And had I not made use of Appogiaturas for Flams, Drags, &c [I] could not have accomplish'd it, but as an Appoggiatura does not partake of any part of the time in such bar—it may be used only as an embellishment."

When we come to this period during which all kinds of published writings became widespread, we begin to have a more detailed idea of the music the fifers and drummers played. The old military traditions were preserved (and to some extent modified) for the new generations of militiamen by numerous publications that put down in writing what had once been an almost completely oral tradition. The field music of the militias developed during these years to become the foundation of the fife and drum corps that have been a part of Connecticut life ever since.

The seminal book of instruction in this phase of the development of the fife and drum was Charles Stewart Ashworth's 1812 book *A New, Useful and Complete System of Drum Beating*. If the title seems hyperbolic in its claim to novelty and thoroughness, it is remarkably modest in its failure to mention that a very useful repertory for the military fife is included. Published in the very new city of Washington in the District of Columbia, for the use of the national army and navy, this manual is more elaborate and complete than most other musical instruction books of its time. Although its instructions are often incomplete sketches of the military music and ceremonies of the day, it would have provided a most useful fleshing out of the instructions given by Von Steuben, and it offers us today a view of military life in the encampments of the new nation.

Each morning the fifes and drums would rouse the encampment with the reveille, which was not merely a brief signal but a series of pieces lasting several minutes in performance. The principal massing of the troops on a typical day was accompanied by the trooping of the colors, and Ashworth also contains one of the few complete and fairly intricate beatings we have for this ceremony (including the singling of the troop, a slow march often in triple meter, sometimes featuring a kind of antiphonal division of the regimental drummers) and the "doublings of the troop," the conclusion of the ceremony, which was a brisk quickstep. In the evening, the tattoo concluded the military day. Ashworth also gives the specific beats (with frustrating ambiguity of notation) for the various calls used to signal daily activities within the camp, as well as signals to warn the soldiers that, for instance, musketry has been heard or the lines of the encampment may have been crossed. Among these were the pioneer's march, "a signal for those on fatigue to turn out—also to Drum out Idle Women from the Camp"; the rogue's march, "used to Drum out Soldiers unworthy to remain in the Service"; as well as expected signals such as "to arms," the "All non Commissioned Officers Call," and a beating whose subsequent history we will look at later, the preparative, which signals "a caution before a Company commences firing, or when on Guard, is beat after the last relief comes in."

The Early New England Fife and Drum Manuals and What They Tell Us

If the Ashworth book represents the U.S. military standard for the fifes and drums, the New England variants on this standard suggest that the militia fifers and drummers of New England were well able to hold their own with the regular troops. Two of the most interesting and thorough of these New England manuals are *The Drummer's Instructor; or, Martial Musician*, by J. L. Rumrille and H. Holton, copyrighted in Vermont and published in Albany in 1817, and the *Massachusetts Collection of Martial Musick*, by Alvan Robinson, Jr., published in Exeter (New Hampshire) in a series of editions (the 1820 second edition seems to have been the most widely distributed). A close analysis of these manuals is not possible here, but a quick glance at some of their salient points will clarify some questions I have frequently heard raised by military reenactors, musicians, and audience members at fife and drum performances.

QUESTION 1:

When was the bass drum introduced to the American military music?

Rumrille and Holton advertised that their book included "instructions for the bass drum," so we can say that by 1817 at least some militia groups had introduced it. The bass drum probably came from Turkey as part of the craze for Janissary music. A fascination for the exotic peculiarities of Middle Eastern culture was a common trope in eighteenth-century Europe; the most famous examples perhaps were Montesquieu's book of political philosophy and manners, *Lettres Persanes* (1721), Mozart's early opera *Die Entführung aus dem Serail* (The Abduction from the Seraglio, 1782), and Beethoven's introduction of the bass drum, triangle, and cymbals as Janissary music in his Ninth Symphony (premiered in 1824). There are reports of big drums being used in military bands in the eighteenth century, but Rumrille and Holton offer the first instruction I know of for the instrument, and their manual is the earliest evidence we have of it being even implicitly included in a military ensemble of fifes and drums.

The bass drum was to be played with one regular drumstick held in the left hand; the right hand held a soft mallet, very much like a modern orchestral mallet: "The right hand stick must not exceed ten inches in length, with a ball at the end six inches in circumference, composed of spunge [*sic*] properly wound with woolen yarn and covered with Cloth or Wash-Leather." Such a short and amply wound mallet could hardly make a sound that would dominate the texture of the ensemble. The examples given of bass drum parts suggest that it was used merely to keep a simple pulse beneath the more intricate snare drum parts. Most unlikely is the instruction that "the Bass Drum must be tuned to chord with the Music with which it plays." Although definite pitch is almost audible on a large and unmuffled bass drum, I have never succeeded in tuning one to the fifes, much less in changing the pitch of the drum when the fifes play a new tune in a different key. What Rumrille and Holton show us, I think, is that the militia units of the early nineteenth century were beginning to think of themselves as the ensembles that would become the fife and drum corps of New England. The New England manuals place less emphasis on the military signals of the drum used in an encampment and provide more examples of marches for both fife and drum. The introduction of the bass drum brings a third element into the ensemble, one that does not make musical sense without the first two.

QUESTION 2:
Did the early American soldier always march slowly?

Not if they were well trained. The manuals clearly indicate both common time marches and quicksteps. Rumrille and Holton are particularly clear on this point, but hardly unique in spelling out at the beginning of the common time repertory "COMMON TIME—75 steps of 2 feet each in a minute," and correspondingly, before the quickstep beatings, "QUICK TIME—120 steps of 2 feet each in a minute." This could hardly be clearer. The confusion comes with regard to the uses of each tempo. While the modern army normally marches at a tempo approximately that of the old quick time, in the eighteenth and early nineteenth centuries the common time cadence was used most frequently, in the manner von Steuben had prescribed during the revolutionary period. The "evolutions," or the soldiers' elaborate maneuvers, were conducted (given an adequate level of skill) at the quickstep, but the common time seems to have been preferred for ceremonial occasions. According to Robinson, "In selecting Marches for the evolutions, Quick time is generally esteemed, except marching in review, into the field, and on to the line, &c. in which cases, Common time should be performed." The quickstep was reserved for its utility in deploying troops rapidly, the common time enabled the troops to march at an easy step, and for most ceremonial occasions.

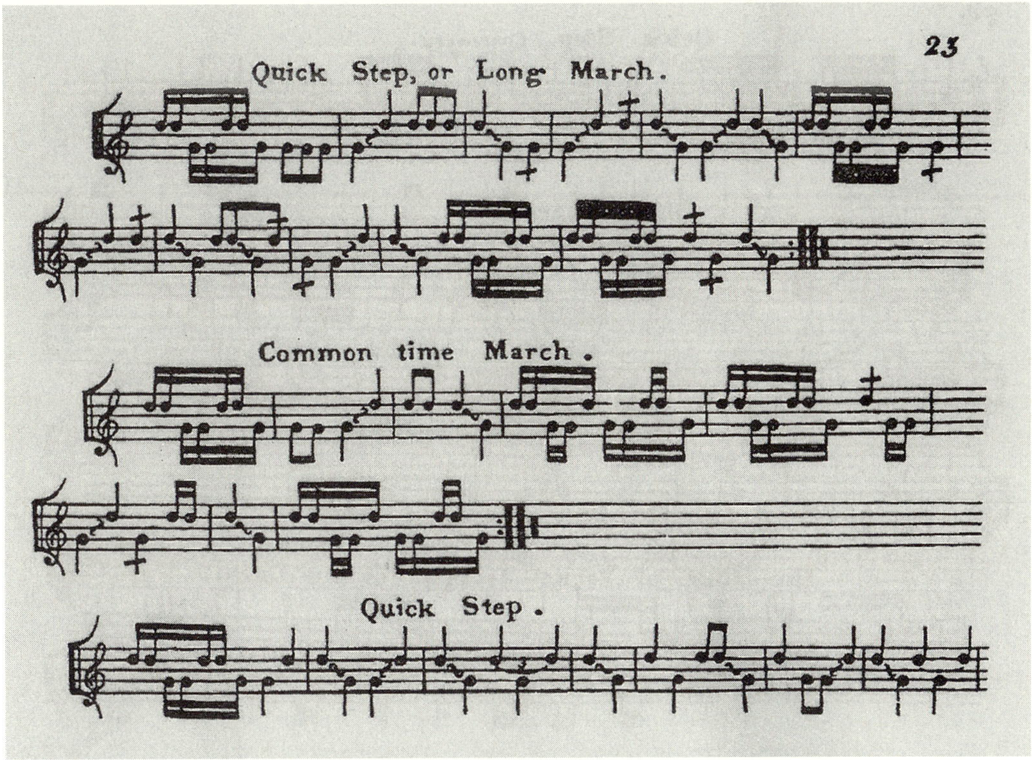

Ashworth's manual, A New, Useful and Complete System of Drum Beating, *offered a type of notation indicating each stroke to be played. The rhythms are not notated, however, despite the appearance of familiar note values. The "Long March" shown on this page was a common beating. Digitally enhanced facsimile courtesy of Edmund W. Boyle*

QUESTION 3:
Were the old-time fifers and drummers good musicians or were they just tapping and tootling along in a country bumpkin or "Yankee Doodle" way?

Surely some of the militia musicians were mere tappers and tootlers, but in all likelihood some were very good performers who had outgrown their purely military function within the militia. As we have seen, in time of war, the able-bodied men who were serviceable soldiers were taken from the fifes and drums to serve in the line. And in times of peace, I find it unimaginable that there weren't companies and battalions who were content, when they met for their rare muster days, with fifers and drummers who hadn't played their instruments since the previous muster day. It seems inescapable to me

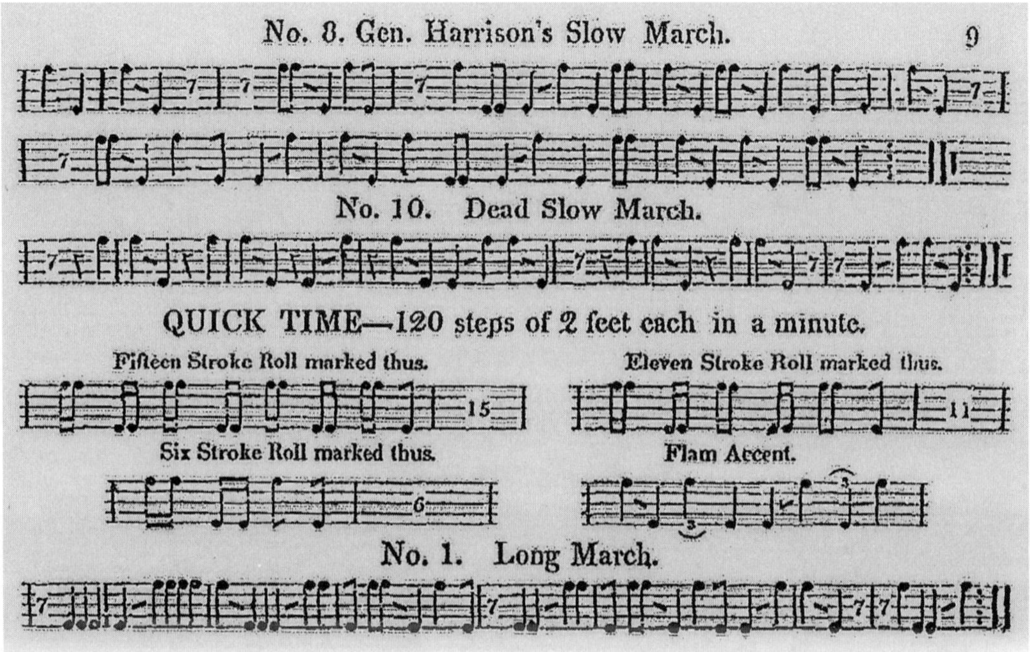

This page from Rumrille and Holton's 1817 Drummer's Instructor *should set to rest the idea that early American martial music should always be played at a slow tempo. The rudiment known as the six-stroke roll, illustrated here, disappeared from the "standard" American drumming rudiments until it regained its popularity among drum and bugle corps in the 1950s, groups that played frequently at 120 steps to the minute. Rumrille and Holton used a slightly different notation from Ashworth's. Rolls are indicated by the number of strokes. The "Long March" shown here is nearly identical to the one shown from Ashworth. Digitally enhanced facsimile by Edmund W. Boyle*

that there was a wide range of skill among the fifers and drummers of the militia. Among the farmers, factory workers, and fishermen who made up the Connecticut militia, there must surely have been many fifers and drummers with little reason or time to practice and perfect their musical performances, and many of the simple duty calls and basic marches can indeed be played with relatively little practice.

Yet there is strong evidence suggesting that more intricate music was also played, music that would have required a commitment to an apprenticeship and practice time far exceeding the requirements of a duty drummer or fifer. For instance, the version of the "College Hornpipe" in Thomas Remington's 1778 manuscript rockets up to D4, above the range of the fife given in any of the military manuals, and features a classical descending sequential

8

Rule 6th.—Where there is a pad-a-diddle or flam-a-diddle performed after a roll, in any beat or march, the hard stroke of the roll should make one of the pad-a-diddle or flam-a-diddle; as the case may be.

OF TIME.

As the drum is an instrument on which the time cannot be so equally and correctly measured as on most other instruments, the greatest caution should therefore be observed in the management of it. For this purpose, the performer should have a general knowledge of the airs, and marches calculated for the different beats of the drum, and their divisions of time; observing in Common and Compound Time to bring down the left foot at the commencement of each bar, and raise it at the middle.—And in Triple Time, to bring down the left foot at the first part, and raise it at the third. At the beginning of a march, (admitting the first bar is full) the hard stroke of the first roll must come down with the first note, but if not, it must come down at the first note of the next bar; for marches, such as are made use of in common martial performances, are generally divided into strains of four, eight, or sixteen bars; so that if the first bar is not full, there are always a sufficient number without it. The performer should always be particular in his performances, observing never to hurry or drag the time, as each are very detrimental to the beat, or march, and appear equally disagreeable to the observer. He should also be particular to beat the rolls as close as possible, and perform them correctly, and the strokes with life and energy; for in doing this, the rests between the strokes and rolls will consequently be longer, which will make it appear much more elegant and intelligible. For where a beat is performed in such a manner as that there is little, or no distinction between the rolls and strokes, none but the best and most competent judges can march after it with any degree of accuracy, without fixing too much of their attention upon the music. For as martial music was instituted entirely for the use, and benefit of Soldiers, the greatest care ought to be observed, not to render its utility abortive by making it unintelligible with unnecessary superfluities. For while they are performing their evolutions, but little of their attention ought to be attached to the music.—It ought, therefore, always to be the study of the musicians, to select such beats, and perform them in such a manner, as shall be best calculated to accomplish the desired effect.

A SELECTION OF BEATS FOR THE DRUM.

Common Time, 1st mode.

1st *Part.*—A seven and three light strokes with the right hand, a flam and three with the left, four flams, stroke three and a two; then a seven and three light strokes with the right hand, a flam and three with the left, a flam, two sevens, and two flams.

The advice in this little essay in Robinson's Massachusetts Collection of Martial Musick *(1818) is still useful. This collection does not use any form of drumming notation but explains the beatings in words, with the understanding that the drummer will know the rhythm and accenting of each rudiment. The first mode of common time here is substantially the same beating given in the pages from Ashworth and from Rumrille and Holton shown earlier, where the beating is called "The Long March." Digitally enhanced facsimile courtesy of Edmund W. Boyle*

pattern in unbroken alla breve eighth notes that lasts for four uninterrupted measures. This is not the kind of thing anyone who hasn't been practicing lately wants to perform.

The manuals give other tantalizing glimpses of unsung (so to speak) resources—techniques and rhythms that some drummers apparently employed. The "Common Time 4th mode, or quick time," in the *Massachusetts Collection of Martial Musick* requires very rapid fifteen-stroke rolls, and some of the common time beatings show quick five-stroke rolls played at the speed of sixty-fourth notes (or possibly a little slower if you distort the rhythm just a little—the score is far from exact). This is not easy. It takes an experienced drummer to play the entire series of quicksteps in *The Drummer's Instructor*, even if the tempo is relaxed somewhat from the indicated 120 beats per minute; the beating for "Jack's Quickstep" is one of the trickiest, with its syncopated paradiddles and run-on phrasing.

But the most demanding and historically resonant instance of advanced drumming is in Rumrille and Holton: a two-strain 6/8 beating called "Double Dragg," which is accompanied by this comment: "N.B. A dragg may be accented to correspond with the air of the fife, and as they are almost entirely neglected, I shall give no further examples." What was this type of "dragg" beating that almost no one played? Well, you have heard something like it before, though probably not from a fife and drum corps. In the 1930s and 1940s, the era of the big bands, the famous drum soloists Chick Webb, Gene Krupa, and Buddy Rich had a favorite technique that never failed to bring down the house: they would play a continuous, rapid, soft roll and punctuate it with carefully placed accented strokes, without disrupting the continuity of the roll. The effect is of two drummers drumming: one plays a soft roll, the other plays an accented rhythm at a higher dynamic level. When the double drag beat is well played, that is exactly the effect—less syncopated than jazz, of course, but "accented to correspond with the air of the fife." Whoever was developing this technique before 1817 was, I can assure you, a more than competent drummer. A very similar double drag beat is found in Potter's *The Art of Beating The Drum*. A likely source for this type of beating is the old tagwacht or reveille beatings of the Swiss and French military drummers.

It was probably music such as these elaborate beatings that so distressed Robinson. Although his *Massachusetts Collection of Martial Musick* (1818) is a wonderful resource of beatings and tunes from the period, it also includes strong and even petulant admonitions to avoid the intricate or merely decorative:

> For as martial music was instituted entirely for the use, and benefit of Soldiers, the greatest care ought to be observed, not to render its utility abortive by making it unintelligible with unnecessary superfluities. For while the soldiers are performing their evolutions, but little of their attention ought to be attached to the music.—It ought, therefore, always to be the study of the musicians, to select such beats, and perform them in such a manner, as shall be the most intelligible to the Soldiers, and add the most beauty and elegance to their evolutions. (9)

What beatings were to be avoided? Well, it seems obvious: exactly those such as Rumrille and Holton's "Jack's Quickstep" or "Double Dragg." Robinson devotes several sentences to a condemnation of exactly the constantly rolling effect the "Double Dragg" is supposed to produce. The passage reads in part: "For where a beat is performed in such a manner as that there is little, or no distinction between the stroke and rolls, none but the best and most competent judges can march after it with any degree of accuracy, without fixing too much of their attention on the music" (9).

The tension between those who employ musicians to provide regular, intelligible, and unsurprising music and those who enjoy the spirit of imagination and creativity in the making of music is very old. Robinson warns his drummers: "It is the duty of the musicians . . . to confine themselves strictly to the system from which they practice; and should never alter any beat or march when performing with others, as it is highly detrimental to its elegance, and renders it unintelligible" (Robinson 1818, 19). There is much to be said in favor of music that is elegant and intelligible, but there is also an aspect of music that values striving to achieve what is complex and novel. It seems clear to me that the militia musicians of the early national period were well acquainted with both of these attitudes toward music.

The Civil War Era

For many years, Connecticut drummers were well known and respected for their "open" military drumming. An early locus of the dissemination of this style seems to have been Middletown. The militia records show that a number of members of the Wilcox family were drum majors in the Sixth Regiment of the Connecticut Militia, which was drawn from the Middletown area. This regiment must have taken their drumming quite seriously. In 1821 a certificate signed by Samuel Wilcox was given to Hezekiah Percival of East Haddam attesting to his skill as a drummer. This list of skills and accomplishments shows a pretty complete comprehension of the rudiments and beatings given in Ashworth's book for the regular army. Percival returned from Middletown with his certificate to the Moodus section of East Haddam and continued drumming. About forty years later, as the election of Abraham Lincoln was triggering the secession of the southern states, Moodus formed its own fife and drum corps, with Hezekiah Percival (and his brother Orville) as their first music instructors. The Moodus Drum and Fife Corps has long been considered the primary link we have to the oldest styles of martial music in New England and remains to this day a testament to the thoroughness of Wilcox's teaching and the tenacity of the Percivals, who preserved this style throughout their long lives and inspired a whole group of youngsters to preserve the old music.

By the time Hezekiah Percival was teaching his Moodus boys to drum in the old style, a new world of military music (now coming to be called

Civil War–era field drum, showing typical artwork, and military fifes. The two fifes with very dark wood are Crosby model Cloos fifes. Instruments courtesy of Museum of Fife and Drum, Ivoryton, Connecticut; photo by Sally Rothenhaus

field music) was developing to lead soldiers into a new style of warfare—technologically advanced, administratively streamlined, and horrific in its effect. We don't know the details of this change in martial music, but the broad picture is fairly clear. According to the music books that survive, the field music of the Civil War was generally quicker and sometimes more intricate than that of previous generations, although the publication of music is far from being conclusive evidence that the music was regularly played. It seems most likely that, as usual, an elite group of fifers and drummers performed some of this more intricate field music and very many more were fortunate if they could play the easiest versions of the duties and marches without serious mishap.

Just as the war created a boom period for victualers, teamsters, and weapons makers, it created an opportunity for the field musicians. Thousands of drums were hurriedly made or refitted to the requirements of the new Union army. Many of them were contracted by the government to be suitable for use by boys rather than men, thus much smaller than the old militia drums the Brown family so carefully crafted in Connecticut. These "contract drums" and others similar to them often had sixteen-inch heads and were perhaps fourteen or twelve inches deep. Instead of the deep, resonant tone of the old militia drums, these new instruments would hold a higher tension more easily (a characteristic of smaller heads) and have a higher, more staccato tone. The fife was also mass-produced during the war. By the end of the war, the Crosby model fife, made in New York by the George Cloos company, set a standard for ease of playing and quality of tone that lasted for a century. These fifes were often two-piece instruments, with a brass tenon connecting the head joint to the body, and the consistency of the machining and attention to detail in construction made them quite easy to play in ensembles.

Much of our knowledge of the actual music played by the field musicians comes to us from the manuals of instruction and repertory that were used during the war. Two of them are of particular interest. One of the most modern reinterpretations of the fife and drum seems to have come from another drummer who trained in Middletown, H. C. Hart, a Civil War colonel, who proclaimed in his advertisement of his instruction manual that he had created "an original system . . . which the author adopted and followed for many years with marked success in teaching, after receiving a thorough practical course of instructions from the Drum Major of the Military Academy at Middletown, Conn., under Professor Patridge." Of the Connecticut drummers I know of, Hart was the first to exert a national influence. His cleverly constructed book has much in it to admire.

First, there is a real attempt to teach beginners, essential at the time because of the huge influx of men into the military. Hart's easy introductory beatings and his fairly comprehensive set of exercises can be useful even today in teaching beginning drummers how to gain control over the fundamentals of their art and provide a basic marching step for parade or maneuvers. His selection of fife tunes similarly offers some that are very simple and that a young fifer could learn within months of taking up the instrument.

Second, Hart provides the fundamentals of the camp duty music very adequately. The various calls and signals are similar to those in Ashworth, and there is some music provided for the slow triple meter troop ceremony, as well as a few common time marches. The "Duke of York's Troop," the most popular trooping tune of all, is given here in fairly sketchy form, with a drum beating much simplified from Ashworth. Clearly, the military music

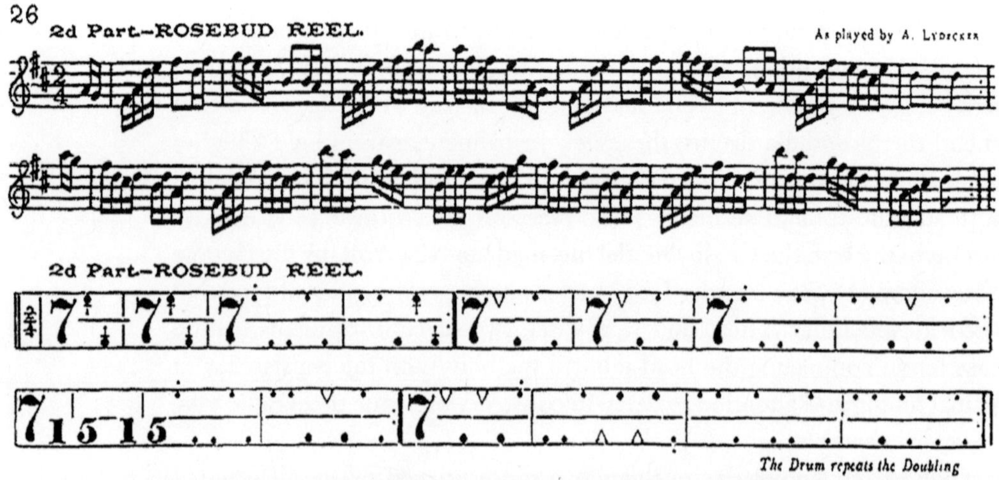

The "Rosebud Reel" in Col. H. C. Hart's manual. This typical Civil War quickstep drum beating, traditionally known as the "Connecticut Halftime," is probably the most familiar of all military American beatings. Digitally enhanced facsimile courtesy of Edmund W. Boyle

that had been the main focus of the eighteenth-century armies was now merely vestigial conventional requirement.

The third and most interesting aspect of Hart's book is his collection of quickstep tunes and drum beatings. Where the earlier books offer a fairly even balance of common time marches and quicksteps, Hart's book is heavily weighted toward the latter. The tunes range from the predictable melodic phrasing and four-square rhythm of marches such as "La Petit Tambour" to numbers taken from minstrelsy such as "Ole Zip Coon." There are also a few wonderful old modal dance tunes. My favorite is "Squirrel Hunter's Quickstep," a 2/4 quickstep with the typical form of two eight-bar strains in the Dorian mode.

Also included is a drum beating that has come to be more closely associated with American rudimental drumming than any other, the beating Hart uses to accompany the "Rosebud Reel" (usually referred to as the "Connecticut Halftime"). It is a straightforward rudimental beating of four strains of four bars each, mostly using rudiments that were introduced in Robinson's 1818 manual. The one exception in it is the drag paradiddle, a composite rudiment that first appears in Potter's book, published in London, but not in any American instruction book earlier than Hart's. The four-strain structure and the drag paradiddles mark this drum beating off from the earlier common time style, although there is nothing here that would have surprised a drummer familiar with Rumrille and Holton's work.

The only publication that transcends the gradual evolution of American fifing and drumming is the *Drummer's and Fifer's Guide*, by George Barrett Bruce and Daniel Decatur Emmett. "Bruce and Emmett," as it is usually called, introduces a level of virtuosity and variety into the repertory of the fifer and drummer that so far exceeds the needs of their military function that it has caused disbelief among musically conservative field musicians that the book was ever used. Emmett was an Ohio-born tunesmith, instrumentalist, and impresario who is primarily remembered for his work bringing the minstrel show to the music hall stage. The banjo-playing "darkie," the rapid patter of comedians working in teams, the sentimental songs and rhythmic dances of the music hall have become an integral aspect of American culture, and Emmett was there at the beginning. During the war, he worked during the day training fifers and drummers at the field music school on Governor's Island in New York harbor. At night he would sometimes take a boat into the city and entertain at the Mechanic's Hall in the show put on by Bryant's Minstrels, for whom he was under contract as a composer. As an active musician who had toured around the country, Emmett knew and worked with many musicians from various backgrounds and in varied styles, and it seems that he felt no need to keep the military music true to its European roots, as it had generally been preserved in New England. He took the extraverted brass band virtuoso style of the then famous cornet soloist Edward Kendall and included in his book a number of pieces using the rapid pedal tone passages, widespread arpeggiations, and some of the harmonic language of the brass bands and transcribed this vocabulary for the fife. Such pieces as "Downshire" and "The Downfall of Paris" show how tunes from the Old World could be dressed up with the high-powered virtuosity of the American band musician, while newly composed marches such as "Newport" and "Ned Kendall's" inaugurate a new direction for the fife. Drum beatings such as those for "Seely Simpkins" and the "Far Down Quickstep" require an analogous virtuosity on the part of the drummers.

With the great recent interest in the Civil War and the reenactment of battles and military evolutions, a great deal of discussion has been aroused and strong opinions expressed concerning Civil War field music. Without going into detailed arguments here, I would suggest the following as a common-sense approach to the field music of the Civil War.

"Newport," a very contemporary-sounding march from The Drummer's and Fifer's Guide, *by George B. Bruce and Daniel Emmett. Photo by Sally Rothenhaus*

There was clearly a tradition of fifing and drumming at a high musical level, at least in the New England states, and possibly throughout the thirteen colonies, from earlier times. Much of the more intricate fifing and drumming of the Civil War period, such as we find in Bruce and Emmett or Hart, is a reasonable extension of the old militia fifing and drumming. Some of this music is quite difficult to play, and it seems clear that there were good players around to play it well.

As far back as the 1830s, the old tempos for marching were being altered. For instance, the 1844 (second) edition of Captain Samuel Cooper's *A Concise System of Instructions and Regulations for the Militia and Volunteers of the United States* makes these changes; they are all in keeping with common sense and experience. The common time step is increased from seventy-five to ninety steps per minute. The new tempo is a very natural easy step for most people, and not a burden to sustain for long periods. The quickstep is reduced from 120 to 110 steps per minute: 120 is quite fast and is difficult to maintain with precision on irregular ground when under pressure. The new step makes it possible to use the quick time more often, and with greater security. (And I believe that the older 120-beat quickstep was honored more in the breach than in the observance, on the basis of my experience in marching and the clear fact that many of the old quickstep drum beatings are very, very awkward to play at 120.) A new time, double quick, is introduced at 140 steps per minute. The trend here is clearly toward the faster tempos, and the quickstep from the pre–Civil War era remained the standard among most Connecticut fife and drum corps into the 1960s.

Melodically, the Civil War–era fifing reflects changes in American society. The old modal tunes that were so common during the revolutionary period are rarer, and often seem to have a self-consciously naive or rustic character. Melodies now often hint, if only slightly, at the harmonic refinements that were the common musical language of the mid-nineteenth century. Tunes from Bruce and Emmett show these developments most clearly. "Newport" and "Fort McHenry," for example, imply secondary dominants through the chromatic inflection of the melodic line, while a march such as "Poor Cato" has a trio section in the relative minor. "Downshire," "Ned Kendall's," and "Major Riley's" are all examples of a kind of virtuoso tradition common to the cornet virtuosos of the period. Rapid pedal tone passages, long runs of arpeggiated chords, and intricate runs such as the succession of broken sixths in "Vinton's Hornpipe" immediately identify the nineteenth-century style of virtuoso wind writing, very different from the occasional earlier use of rapid figuration such as we have seen in the classical scale-based sequential patterns in Remington's 1778 "College Hornpipe."

The drumming of the Civil War period offers many examples of a busier style that I think of as quickstep drumming. I will explain. Eighteenth-century drumming often fills up entire measures with single taps, often one or two taps per marching step (quarter or eighth notes in common modern notation). This is a very good, uncluttered way to keep time for marching. On every marching step, or often only on the left foot, the drummer would play a flam, which consists of playing with both sticks at almost the same time. These flams reinforce and emphasize the beat. Rudiments that fill in more than these basic divisions of the marching measure are used sparingly, and Robinson would have considered them unnecessary complications. In most of the Civil War–era beatings, these flams are no longer placed to provide accents but are simply the norm: any unadorned tap that is an eighth note or longer in a quickstep automatically becomes a flam. Indeed, when I first started playing some of the older drum beatings, I found it a strange sensation to play taps that were not flams, and whenever I write a beating for a group of drummers and include some unadorned eighth notes, I am invariably asked if I had meant to write them as flams, so pervasive is the tendency to add some ornament to every tap.

Fifers and drummers who wish to shy away from the extraverted and virtuosic style of the more elaborate pieces in Hart and Bruce and Emmett are, historically, on solid ground. A great deal of the Civil War–era music is simpler than these pieces, and quick-fingered fifers have rifled these books only for the purpose of extracting the most virtuosic works in them. Performing the full breadth of the Civil War repertory, from simple to complex, including the remaining common time marches and troops as well as some of the virtuoso quicksteps, would make an excellent concert of military music.

In the early national period, American military music began to assume a national identity. From the militia music books of the early years of the nineteenth century through the field music of the Civil War era, our separation from European culture, as in so many other aspects of American life, became evident. By 1865, when the soldiers began to return home after the Civil War, they had in their imaginations a kind of music for fifes and drum that was now uniquely American, moving at a bright, quickstep tempo, taking its cues in part from the active American culture that surrounded it, the brass bands, the minstrel shows, even (as we will see) the circus. In Connecticut, some of the stalwart champions of the old militia music, distrustful of these new sounds from far away, resisted these new influences. As the fife and drum tradition in Connecticut continued after the Civil War, the old militia common time marches and the newly popular quicksteps would create rival factions, both of which were called "Ancient."

4

THE CONNECTICUT FIFERS AND DRUMMERS ASSOCIATION

THE CIVIL WAR ENDED in April 1865, and thereafter the fife and drum rapidly diminished in importance in the United States military, to be replaced by the bugle and the military band. But the mass mobilization of the Civil War had broadened the public's interest in all things military, including field music. In the last decades of the nineteenth century, fife and drum corps as well as other local musical organizations abounded throughout the United States, and in Connecticut the remains of the old militia music made a starting point for many of these organizations.

But removed from its military function, the fife and drum repertory changed. The pieces in slow triple meter that had long been part of the trooping of the colors were dispensed with among the local corps. The "duty music" or "calls" that regulated the day of a military encampment were also lost. Such music had no place in the world of ceremonial parades and civic functions. Similarly, the distinction between common time marches and quicksteps was no longer useful. Few things disrupt a local parade more effectively than having the drum corps alter its marching tempo by thirty or forty steps per minute along the parade route.

All of these losses meant a diminution in the color and interest of the fife and drum repertory, made inevitable by the change in the instruments' status. Today, as some historically oriented fifers and drummers seek to recapture parts of the older fife and drum experience, this lost repertory is being researched anew. But in the late nineteenth century, these niceties only stood in the way of having a successful drum corps.

Much of the loss of repertory is a result of the increasing uniformity of the quickstep tempo in military music. There is a substantial practical difficulty in having to perfect a variety of marching tempi. The difficulty of playing much faster than normal is obvious, but the marching problem is more subtle. People generally like to walk at about one hundred steps per minute or a little faster. Try this experiment: stride off purposefully, but not in a hurry, carrying a moderately loaded backpack, wearing heavy shoes, and after five minutes or so, evaluate the speed of your stride. I bet that it will be around 110 steps per minute, give or take 10 steps per minute. This is just about the speed of the Civil War–era quickstep, and it is a comfortable tempo. Most of the Connecticut fife and drum corps seem to have settled into this tempo for their marching (though definitive evidence is not easy to find). But a few of them, most notably the Moodus Drum and Fife Corps, concentrated on the common time marches (seventy-five to ninety steps per minute) that had been the fundamental repertory of the militia fifers and drummers. Some new music crept into the repertory of even these corps in the late nineteenth century, tunes such as "Grandfather's Clock" and "Golden Slippers." But just as everything touched by the legendary King Midas turned to gold, everything Moodus played became a common time march.

The fife and drum corps of Connecticut came to be divided into three categories, a taxonomy most easily differentiated by the varieties in marching tempo. The "Modern" corps, unfortunately not the subject of this book but including corps like the famous St. Peter's corps of Torrington, played at 120 steps to the minute. (A note on names: it is difficult if not impossible to provide official names for many fife and drum corps; many of them are never aware of their official names, which may only exist for legal purposes, should a corps have legal status. With a few exceptions—Moodus Drum and Fife Corps, Mattatuck Drum Band, New York Regimental Fife and Drum Band—all the groups have an official name ending with Fife and Drum Corps—but no one refers to them by these long titles.) The "Ancient" corps, particularly those who played in the contests held by the Connecticut Fifers and Drummers Association (CF&DA)—such as the Lancraft Fife and Drum Corps from North Haven and the local corps of Yalesville, North Branford, and Stony Creek—played at about 110 steps per minute. And then there were the old-time Ancient corps, such as the Moodus Drum and Fife Corps, that played between seventy-five and ninety steps per minute. The Modern corps and the competitive Ancient corps generally came from the busier, more economically advanced areas of the state, while the "old-time" Ancient corps came from the smaller towns, and so a survey of Connecticut's drum corps heritage becomes an excursus on the state's geography and industry.

In the nineteenth century, water power was used in many factories, and water transportation was an important means of distributing manufactured goods. The Connecticut River, trending southward through the center of the state, proved a critical resource and a focal point for much of Connecticut's early development. Springfield, Massachusetts, located near the river just above the Connecticut border, was an active drum corps town, and among the Springfield factories was the famous Springfield armory. Strongly linked to the nation's military history, the armory was established as a national arsenal during the Washington administration, and produced the famous Springfield muskets of the Civil War, and the classic Springfield 1903-A3 rifle, continuing to produce arms through the Vietnam era. Moving downstream from Springfield, other drum corps towns included Enfield, also a center of much manufacturing, Windsor (famous for its tobacco farms), and the state's capital, Hartford. Hartford was settled by the Dutch, who came up from New York and the Hudson River around 1631 to take advantage of the settlement's important location on the river. (Hart, or deer, could ford or cross over the river in the shallow water there, and a hart ford was a good river crossing for humans as well.)

Wethersfield, just south of Hartford, is the home of Connecticut's oldest church (the First Church of Wethersfield), as well as the state's oldest junior fife and drum corps, named after the revolutionary hero Colonel John Chester. Middletown, in the center of the state, was of course the center of drum instruction for many militia drummers under Samuel Wilcox, whom we have met. Moving down the river valley to the coast, the population thins out again (the bustling city of New Haven, located on the Long Island sound, dominated development in the lower Connecticut River valley. (New Haven's favorable location is, like Hartford's, etymologically revealed, for "haven" means both a safe place and a harbor—from the German *hafen*, or harbor.) The Connecticut River joins with the sea at Old Saybrook (from "sea brook," or estuary), but with the help of the railroads, the harbor of New Haven, several miles to the west, formed the main traffic route.

As the railways made transportation of manufactured goods quicker and cheaper throughout the nineteenth century, the western hills of Connecticut became an important manufacturing region. The earlier farming communities located in these hills provided a stable but not an easy living. With the coming of the factories, plentiful jobs led to rapid population increase. The

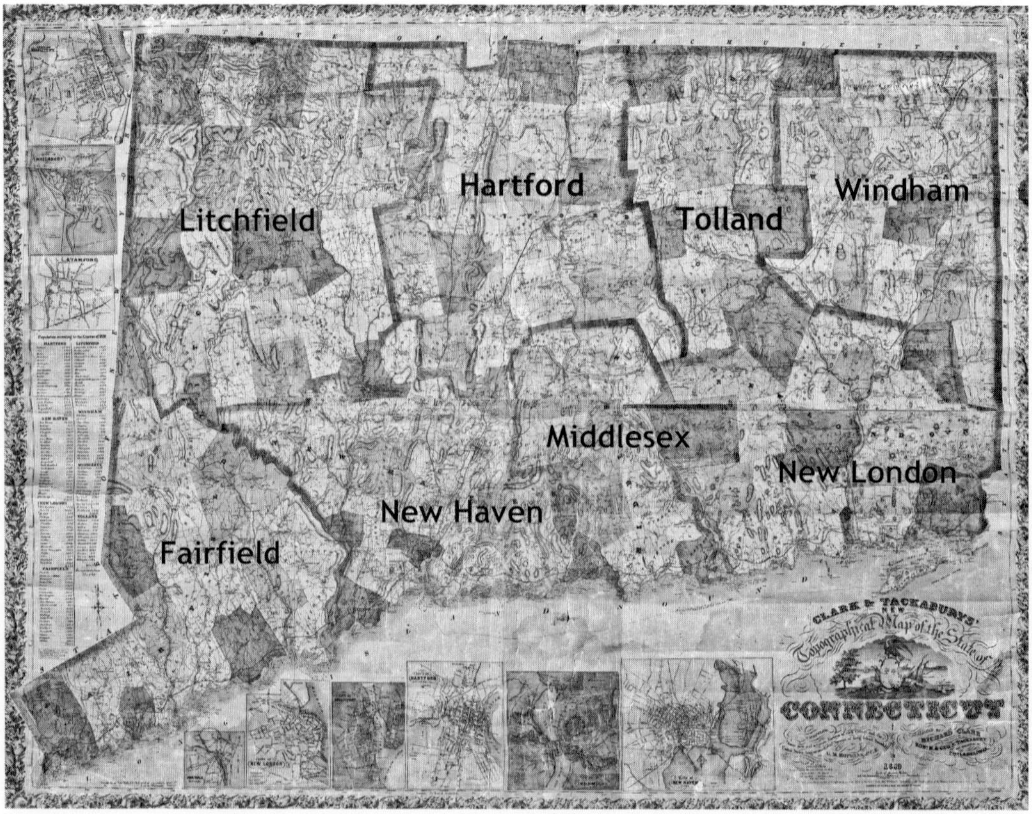

The most active region for the competitive drum corps was to the west of the Connecticut River, from Hartford County into Litchfield County, moving out toward the western hills.

new, industrial working class was the basis for the area's social activities, which included community bands and drum corps. Driving through Litchfield County today, you can readily see these historical developments. The old farming life is evoked in the extremely beautiful county seat of Litchfield, even today characterized by a slow pace of life. Lazing on Litchfield's beautiful, shaded town green on a summer's day, surrounded by historic homes and beautiful farms and forests, it is easy to imagine how the town may have looked when the once notorious Aaron Burr, vice president during the Jefferson administration, studied in law offices here. But a short drive north on Route 202 takes you to Torrington, located on the fast-running Naugatuck River, a perfect instance of the Connecticut factory town. The town center is a cluster of multifamily residences and shops. Some of the old factory buildings are still visible, and the well-maintained sidewalks and parks suggest a town where people like to go out and socialize with their neighbors. When the Great Depression hit this manufacturing town, the local Catholic Church, St. Peter's, formed a drum corps to provide an outlet for the children of the town. Eighty years later, having won thousands of awards, and performed internationally dozens of times, the proud St. Peter's Modern corps (one of the rare ones today, with fifes, drums, and brass instruments) continues to serve as a local institution. If the town of Litchfield recalls the agrarian dreams of a colonial period dominated by the small farmstead, the Congregational church, and the village green, Torrington suggests a later American experience, when immigrants came to an already established United States looking for work and maybe a little prosperity for themselves and their children, and dare we say it, a special kind of liberty that they came to find in this new world.

It was largely within the quadrangle whose endpoints are roughly Hartford, Middletown, New Haven, and Torrington that the CF&DA flourished for nearly a century (although towns as far west as Bridgeport, Danbury, and Bethel also contributed regularly to it). The many industrial towns in this region, particularly Waterbury, Bristol, and Meriden, all fielded many drum corps during the heyday of the CF&DA. These competitive corps from the more populous and forward-looking part of the state developed a musical style influenced by the quickstep music of the Civil War. Various drumming contests were held in the state, many rather loosely organized, until in 1885 the CF&DA was established to sanction contests and to prescribe the standards of fifing and drumming to its member groups. In the early years these standards were quite loose, and judges were chosen more for their prominence in the community than for their musical knowledge.

In those days before recorded music, when professional ensembles were rarely heard, a drum corps contest was a holiday, with a noisy, festive parade and an afternoon of music played on a town green or perhaps a ball field. The competing corps generally consisted of ten to twenty-four musicians. The decision to compete in a contest was often casually made at the last minute, and the group of local fellows who made up the corps would play their regular parade pieces at the contest. Today's drum and bugle corps and marching band contests are a direct outgrowth of these events, but the atmosphere is quite different. Today's big groups spend hundreds of thousands of dollars annually on national tours, the services of professional music arrangers, choreographers, and instrumental and marching instructors, and they change their uniforms and even their instruments frequently, sometimes from year to year. The contemporary fan of these groups is used to spending large amounts on tickets and travel to the large football stadiums where the contests are held.

A newspaper account of the 1885 State Convention expresses the spirit of the time, the naive enthusiasm, and the satirical hyperbole. As Shakespeare knew, the fife and drum create both majestic ceremony and Dionysian tumult, and when these instruments are separated from their strict military function, onlookers often can't decide whether they should respect the musicians or mock them—grown men and women dressing up in costume and banging on drums and shrieking on fifes is perhaps not something to be taken entirely seriously. The following newspaper account of 1885 was reprinted with some bemusement by the CF&DA itself when it celebrated its seventy-fifth anniversary in 1960:

WALLINGFORD INVADED
Twenty-one Drum Corps Made the Air Hideous
The Sassacus Corps of New Haven
Carried Off First Prize
People Gathered From Near And Far

It will be weeks before this village will recover from the shock it has experienced today. There has been nothing like it since the tornado of '78, seven years ago, carried the Cony House on Wallace Road over into the Connecticut River Valley depositing it there and then coming back after the town clerk. The experience of today has been more disastrous than a scourge of 17 year locusts. We have suffered from a scourge of drummers and their visitation not from the mild form of commercial drummer, but the most virulent type of military drummer. What accursed fatality made the drum corps of the state elect the quiet little village of Wallingford for their first state convention will never be known. But whatever the motive was it is sufficient that they came and kept the village terrorized from morn to dewy eve.

They descended on us from both railroads, the New York, New Haven and Hartford and also the airline [term used for an efficient railway route: the shortest distance between two points] in the eastern part of town. They poured in on foot, on wagons from every road leading into the town. They brought fifers with them to add to the torture and the result was as if a thousand boiler shops were in operation all at the same time with a man filing a saw before each one of them.

Twenty-one of these gangs of desperadoes or drum corps as they called themselves—came from as many different cities and villages including New Haven, Hartford, Danbury, Meriden, Waterbury, Moodus, Mansfield, Ansonia, Guilford, Birmingham, Windsor, Waterville, Middletown, Northford, Derby, Stony Creek, and various other localities. Numbering over three hundred each with an instrument of torture.

They showed no mercy for sex or age and they poured their din alike on the ears of the just and the unjust. The police were so intimidated that they even escorted the invaders around many of the streets of our village.

By noon the entire force of drum corps from all over the state had arrived and pandemonium reigned. The din of the invaders brought the people from all the country round to ascertain what was the matter and there were long trains of carriages, wagons, sulkies, buck-board, "Spindles," foggies and every other species of vehicle tending towards the village upon every road that entered it from east, west, north and south.

Not satisfied with the violent entrance into the unhappy village, the invaders add insult to injury, by flaunting themselves through the principal streets in a shameless, but gaudy and glittering procession which the affrighted inhabitants even affected to admire, and crowded out onto the sidewalk to admire.

It seemed as if the whole population of Wallingford, Meriden and the surrounding towns was in the village. Every man, woman and child, even the dogs all being in attendance. All along the Main Street booths had arisen where the same [*sic*] of ham sandwiches, ginger pop and even those drinks that lure to ruin were sold. The pitiless invaders headed by Colonel Leavenworth on horseback began their march at noon, one drum corps following another in a long and glittering procession that took fifty minutes to pass a given point.

Haughty drum majors['] lofty bear skins, high upon their proud heads marched backwards before their various commands, scintillating with brass buttons and gold braid. Tall drummers and short drummers with thin potato mashers. Great and small fifers, fifed mercilessly and abandoned cymbalists added to the clattering thunder, so that the noise shook green apples off the trees, loosened the nails in shingles on roofs and eggs out of hens in poultry houses, along the line of march. The villagers attempted to propitiate the invaders by spreading long tables with a bountiful lunch at the City Rink Grove overlooking Community Lake.

After getting the entire village coralled in the rink enclosure they proceeded to extract a dime ransom from each and every one. The drummers began their orgies and so strange a thing as [*sic*] human nature that children laughed and played. Young people carried on flirtatiously or chatted together while their elders discussed domestic matters, the crops, price of pigs, etc. while the awful preparations were being made. Finally the awful truth, came upon them with a sickening force, that the drummers were about to enter upon a competitive trial for prizes in their presence. The judges were balloted upon in the horse sheds.

Drum Major William E. Boole and William A. Green of Meriden and Charles Hendricks of Wallingford were chosen. These three judges sat with their backs to the drummers so there could be no partiality shown. The different corps were chosen in the order their numbers were drawn from a derby hat. The hideous rites began with a performance by the Merwin corps of New Haven, consisting of ten boys in drab uniforms assisted by a wizened and gray headed man who was old enough to know better, they banged and tooted away for five minutes then retired, each of the other 20 corps came along in the order they were drawn.

As shades of evening began to settle over the old rink their orgies came to an end, each winning drum corps receiving their prize. They then marched to the railroad station still thumping, banging, flutting [fluting?], piccoling, and cymbaling, followed by the entire village.

Special trains finally carried them away, ending the first organized Drummers Convention of the State of Connecticut.

The big city corps, relatively speaking, tended to dominate the prizes in those formative years, and a corps that had a sponsoring organization was often more successful than the local groups that were just collections of local fellows (in the early years, all corps were composed of men). Factory workers, as a group, were particularly avid in drum corps competitions, often joining with coworkers to field a corps from their own shop. Were their hours spent in the factory not enough for them? But we should remember that for most of these working-class men, their factory's drum corps offered their only opportunity to have contact with any kind of music teacher or learn about music or perform in any kind of ensemble. Several corps were organized in Hartford, including one representing the Colt Firearms Company, but perhaps the most famous of the factory corps was the Royal Typewriter Company's corps of Hartford, organized in 1918, whose members practiced on the factory floor, falling into formation between the large metalworking machines. Decades later, they proudly reported in a CF&DA history in 1960 that "in the original corps, only one man was familiar with fifing and drumming and out of raw material, the two instructors built up a corps that won its initial prize a little more than a year late in a state competition." Another factory corps that had success in the early years was the American Graphophone corps from Bridgeport. This company's product, the Graphophone, was in direct competition with Thomas Edison's better known Gramophone sound recording and playback instruments. Frank Fancher, who won the individual drumming championship a record eight times in the early part of the twentieth century, started off with this Bridgeport corps.

The Ancient corps were less likely to have this type of sponsorship, perhaps because the activity of drummers and fifers sometimes long predated the large factories and their organization of workers' groups. For instance, one of the charter members of the CF&DA was the Mattatuck Drum Band, whose history is traced directly back to 1767, when musicians for the local (Farmingbury) trainband had a fife and drum accompaniment, which later became the famous Wolcott Drum Band, and then, moving to Waterbury, the Mattatuck Drum Band, still active today. The Yalesville Fife and Drum Corps, competing in the Ancient class since 1911, was also part of a long local tradition. Yalesville is a section of the town of Wallingford (whose first town drummer we met in chapter 1). Rope tension drums have been played in Wallingford for over three hundred years. I was active as a drum instructor to the very fine Yalesville senior ancient Corps as recently as 2006, and the corps continues to perform today.

Some corps are only listed by the name of their leader, often a factory owner who organized a corps for his workers. W. B. Bunnell's corps is one of these, first listed in the very earliest years of the CF&DA. Bunnell's corps was from Northford, a tiny section of North Branford, just outside New Haven. Frank Bunnell himself placed high among the individual snare drummers throughout the 1890s, but the corps didn't gain its first snare drum individual championship until they (apparently) moved their location to the big city of New Haven. In 1901 and 1902 George Chidsey of Bunnell's claimed the championship.

Many of the corps, of course, had a few moments at their peak when they won many awards and then faded back out of view, while a few corps, such as the Lancraft corps, from North Haven (adjacent to New Haven), stayed

The Royal Typewriter corps was one of many Modern corps sponsored by Connecticut manufacturing companies. The Royal Typewriters were for many years an internationally distributed product, and the corps, mostly composed of employees, used to practice right on the factory floor in Hartford.
Photo in author's collection

consistently active in CF&DA politics and competition, taking home dozens of trophies over several decades. Like many corps of the time, Lancraft was affiliated with a business, in this case, an oyster merchant Ed Lancraft, who donated the original uniforms in 1888 and who has been honored ever since with the name of one of Connecticut's most respected and long-lived Ancient corps. Over the years, Lancraft has boasted a very stable roster. Once in the corps, people tend to stay. One of the early individual champion drummers who played with Lancraft was Earl Sturtze, whose influence on the history of rudimental drumming in the United States was decisive for decades. Fairly early in his adult life, Sturtze was able to give up the factory work in which—like most drum corps drummers—he was employed and established a teaching studio for rudimental drumming that became his life's work.

The great longtime rival to Lancraft in the Ancient class was the Stony Creek Fife and Drum Corps. Like Lancraft, Stony Creek was organized in the 1880s, and they are geographically close to each other; a little village only a few miles up the coast from New Haven, Stony Creek was occupied in those days by fishermen and quarry workers. Lancraft won more than two dozen state titles between 1909, its first title, and 1969, its final title. So far. But Stony Creek won six consecutive Ancient titles in the 1930s, a feat that, I believe, Lancraft never matched. Perhaps from this recitation of statistics you can begin to grasp the massive seriousness associated with winning at the State Meet, or State Convention, as it was called, to differentiate it from the various "field days"—the lesser contests throughout the year. These contests provided a focus for the practice of the corps and individuals and, ideally at least, rewarded the performers who perfected their art to the highest level.

The rivalries sometimes led to developments within the corps. The famous teacher of drumming, historian of drumming, drum maker, and avid drummer Sanford A. "Gus" Moeller, came up from New York for several years to play with the Lancraft corps. Stony Creek later hired Sturtze as drum teacher, who had taught, I am tempted to say produced, so many of the excellent Lancraft drummers. Stony Creek bought a beautiful set of large drums (with eighteen-inch heads) in the 1930s. Lancraft commissioned a set of drums from Gus Moeller, with smaller seventeen-inch heads but extra deep and with ornate paintings on them.

More important than winning contests, each corps had a characteristic sound. I was not around when these corps were in their competitive prime, but each retained its characteristic approach for many years after the period when winning the State Meet was the focal point of every summer. More than thirty-five years ago, as a member of the Connecticut Yanks of Bristol, I did compete against both the Lancraft and Stony Creek corps. The famous drum line of Lancraft looked like a line of Sturtze individual competitors, which it was. The "height and rise" of the sticks (as the judging sheet termed the uniformity of the drummers' motions) was immaculate, and the fortissimos were very, very loud. The fife parts were quite simple, even by the standards of the day, but the sheer excellence of the snare drum section could never be ignored. Measure after measure of immaculately executed rudiments in nearly perfect unison rolled by, all delivered with the most relaxed certainty that the next roll, like all of those before, would also be beautifully timed and gracefully executed. The Stony Creek sound, I have always thought, balanced the bass and the snares with the fife a little more carefully. The fife parts, while not complex, were often interesting combinations of reels and jigs, and the overall effect was less one of watching perfection than

The Lancraft Fife and Drum Corps (c. 1960)—perhaps the most active Ancient competitive corps in the history of the Connecticut Fifers and Drummers Association. Lancraft was always known as a drummers' corps, and many of the most famous drummers have been associated with the corps, including Hugh Quigley, Earl Sturtze, Gus Moeller, and many, many others. Photo in author's collection

of watching folk musicians having a very good time playing well. In addition, each of these corps produced any number of fine drummers and fifers, many of whom went on to start other corps, become expert teachers, or simply become very good role models for the younger people coming up through the ranks. From the 1880s through the 1950s, Connecticut seemed to be awash with expert quickstep fifers and "open-style" drummers, while the rest of the country had shifted to the Modern, closed style of drumming and replaced the fife with the bugle.

In these early years the rules were very simple, and judging was somewhat relaxed, with corps and individual scores artificially high, winning competitors often scoring in the range of ninety-six out of one hundred or even higher. And the basis of judging was already diverging from the origin of the drum corps as provider of martial music. As we have seen, in the military, the essential criterion of a marching piece is its tempo, and two types predominated, the slow or common time march, and the quickstep. By 1892, the CF&DA specified that two pieces were to be played by each

The drum section of the Stony Creek Drum Corps. This photo was probably taken while in competition at the 1940 New York World's Fair. Photo in author's collection

competing corps, but the distinction between the two was not one of tempo but of meter: one 2/4 and one 6/8 piece were required. This distinction is nearly meaningless to marching soldiers but of practical interest to the performers, particularly to those who are fans of Irish dance music. The reel and the hornpipe are (approximately) 2/4 dances, and a jig is normally a 6/8. (A subcategory called the slip jig is normally written in 9/8.) Not all corps played reels and hornpipes for their 2/4 piece, but the vast majority of 6/8s I have ever heard in Connecticut have been jigs, usually of Irish origin. Again, as early as 1892 there were categories for different styles of corps—Ancient and Modern and with drums only (!)—and a category for piccolo and flute corps.

Solo performances, or "individual" contests, always played a large role at these events. The favorite virtuosos were remembered from year to year and made reputations that enthusiasts recalled for generations. In individuals, fifers were required to play one 2/4 piece and one 6/8. Details of these competitions are scarce, but the best Ancient fifers often played the Crosby model Cloos fifes, which have a clear tone in the upper register and a very fast response, enabling the fifer to articulate the rapidly tongued passages commonly found in Irish reels and the quicksteps popularized in "the Bruce Book," as many old-timers usually called Bruce and Emmett's *Drummer's and Fifer's Guide*. The Civil War veterans organization, the Grand Army of the Republic (GAR), published a small booklet of tunes, *The American Veteran Fifer*, in 1905, many of which have become favorites for fifers in competition ever since. All tunes are written in keys with one, two, or three sharps, to facilitate intonation, and nearly all notes are tongued; slurred passages occur very rarely. Included are dozens of quicksteps in both 2/4 and 6/8. A few are quite easy and attractive melodies, such as "The Croquette," "Ed Kellog's Q.S. [quickstep]," "Guilderoy" (Irish for "the red-haired boy"), and "Finnegan's Wake." Some of the more difficult pieces have become standard virtuoso vehicles for accomplished fifers, such as "Dashing White Sergeant" and "Corn Cob Clog." *The American Veteran Fifer* also has a slightly different type of quickstep featuring nearly constant sixteenth-note figurations, occasionally broken up by ragtime-like syncopations. Two of my favorites of this type are "Major J. N. Bogart's Banquet" and "Denman Duncan's Drumbeat" (the compiler had a deeply regrettable urge to create alliterative titles). Some tunes from this book that have become standard repertory among fife and drum corps include "The Jaybird," "Fireman's Quickstep," and "Ricketts Hornpipe."

Many of the tunes in both Bruce and Emmett and *The American Veteran Fifer* are quite difficult, and very few corps have attempted them. Throughout the history of the CF&DA it was common for even quite good corps to play simple jigs (such as "The Irish Washerwoman" or the very popular "Sisters" jig). In the 1950s, for example, the famous North Branford corps played for their 2/4 selections "Dixie," "Caledonia," or "Swanee River," all favorites of the time.

For drummers, the full corps favorites were "straight" rudimental drumming quicksteps like those found in Bruce and Emmett or Hart. In individual competition, the drummers also distanced themselves from the traditional requirements of military drummers. The sine qua non of the military drummer is a secure knowledge of the duty calls and signals. For the new drum corps drummers, or "rudimentalists," who never played in a military encampment, these duty calls were meaningless. Instead, the rudiments of drumming, or the "rules," as Percival and Pete Mietzner of the Moodus corps called them, gained new importance. No longer merely elementary exercises to be practiced as a practical means of developing skills, the rudiments in Connecticut became an end in themselves.

Drummers from all over the country, and even from Europe, have heard a great deal about the "Twenty-Six Standard American Drum Rudiments," a peculiarly fictitious term. Here is how this idea came to be. In 1869, the U.S. army adopted a new manual, *Strube's Drum and Fife Instructor*, by Gardiner Strube, who had served during the war in Duryea's Zouaves, of the Fifth Regiment of New York Volunteers. This manual received wide distribution and became the most common resource for drummers in the Northeast (and probably throughout the country) for many decades after the war. Strube eliminated some of the most interesting rudiments from earlier drumming manuals and reduced the number from over thirty (as found in Bruce and Emmett, in itself a truncation of earlier manuals) to twenty-five. Later drummers added the single roll (a rapid succession of notes, one tap in each hand: left, right, left, right, etc.). These twenty-six came to be called the Standard American Drum Rudiments.

It was the twenty-five Strube rudiments that were used for the Connecticut contests. Patterns that had been used in, say, Ashworth (1812), such as the treble paradiddle, or the very useful four-stroke ruff found in Robinson (1818), were not included in Strube, nor were other useful rudiments such as the roll of eight strokes, the side flamadiddle, and the full drag. In addition, the accenting was often simplified in the older rudiments that were retained. For instance, the flamacue, first introduced in Bruce and Emmett (1862) and not found earlier in either a rudiment list or in a published beating, became a "Standard American Rudiment," with two of the three accents indicated in Bruce and Emmett now eliminated.

In short, Strube was a contemporary resource, no doubt accurately reflecting the drumming of the New York Zouaves with whom Strube played, but far from an encyclopedic representation of the American tradition. Because of its publication after the war's end and the great rise in popularity of drum corps in the late nineteenth century, Strube became the standard drumming book (there is very little fifing to be found in it). And so the whole history of American military drumming from colonial days through the Civil War became an increasingly lost musical style, except for the small remnants preserved in Strube's newly authoritative manual. In recent decades, when the Percussive Arts Society undertook their own standardization of drumming rudiments (an ongoing project) it was as an updating of the Strube list.

When the rudiments were played at a contest (and in the early days sometimes as many as five different rudiments would be played by each individual), they were "run down" for the judge: begun at a "dead slow" tempo (usually about forty beats per minute) and gradually accelerated until after about a minute and a half the drummer was playing at full speed. This is called "closing" the rudiment. Then came a gradual ritardando, taking about the same amount of time, until the end was played at about the same speed as the beginning ("opening" the rudiment). The closest popular parallel to running down rudiments is the practice of performing the school figures at figure skating competitions—required patterns that for decades were performed as a measure of the contestant's technical control and precision, not of artistic creativity or individuality. Both school figures and running down rudiments are now pretty much lost skills, and flashy programs

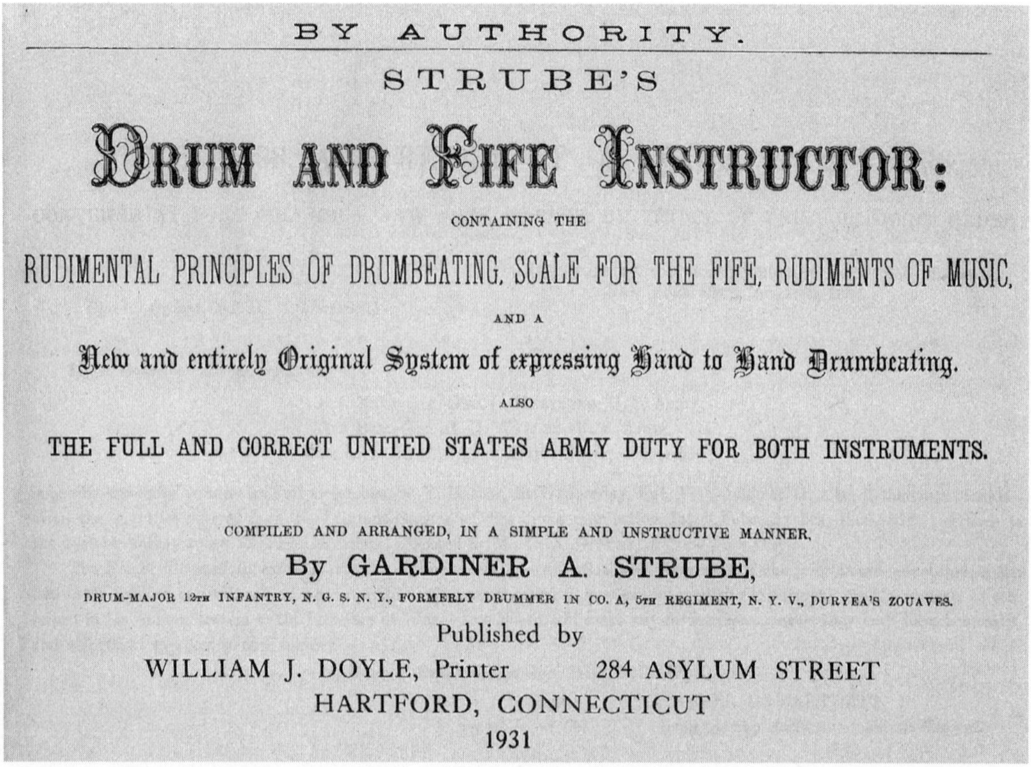
BY AUTHORITY.

STRUBE'S

DRUM AND FIFE INSTRUCTOR:

CONTAINING THE

RUDIMENTAL PRINCIPLES OF DRUMBEATING, SCALE FOR THE FIFE, RUDIMENTS OF MUSIC,

AND A

New and entirely Original System of expressing Hand to Hand Drumbeating.

ALSO

THE FULL AND CORRECT UNITED STATES ARMY DUTY FOR BOTH INSTRUMENTS.

COMPILED AND ARRANGED, IN A SIMPLE AND INSTRUCTIVE MANNER,

By GARDINER A. STRUBE,

DRUM-MAJOR 12TH INFANTRY, N. G. S. N. Y., FORMERLY DRUMMER IN CO. A, 5TH REGIMENT, N. Y. V., DURYEA'S ZOUAVES.

Published by

WILLIAM J. DOYLE, Printer 284 ASYLUM STREET

HARTFORD, CONNECTICUT

1931

The Connecticut Fifers and Drummers Association paid to have the Strube manual republished in Hartford so that all drummers would have the same list of rudiments to practice. Photo in author's collection

designed to appeal to more dramatic instincts in an audience now prevail in both sorts of competition.

In addition to the rudiments, in those early days each drummer played two pieces. According to all reports, none of the pieces required as much skill as the running down of the rudiments. The third requirement in the individual competition was for the drummer to play the "Three Camps," the opening sequence of the old army reveille. The "Three Camps" was chosen, drummers agree, not for its historical military significance but because it provides a good way of judging the finesse and clarity of the drummer's most important rudiment, the long roll.

"Time" and "execution" were the watchwords of the judges. "Time" meant how close to the prescribed Ancient tempo of 110 beats per minute the individual or corps could keep (120 for Modern corps). "Execution" meant the clarity of the performance. For instance, a roll that was "rubbed,"

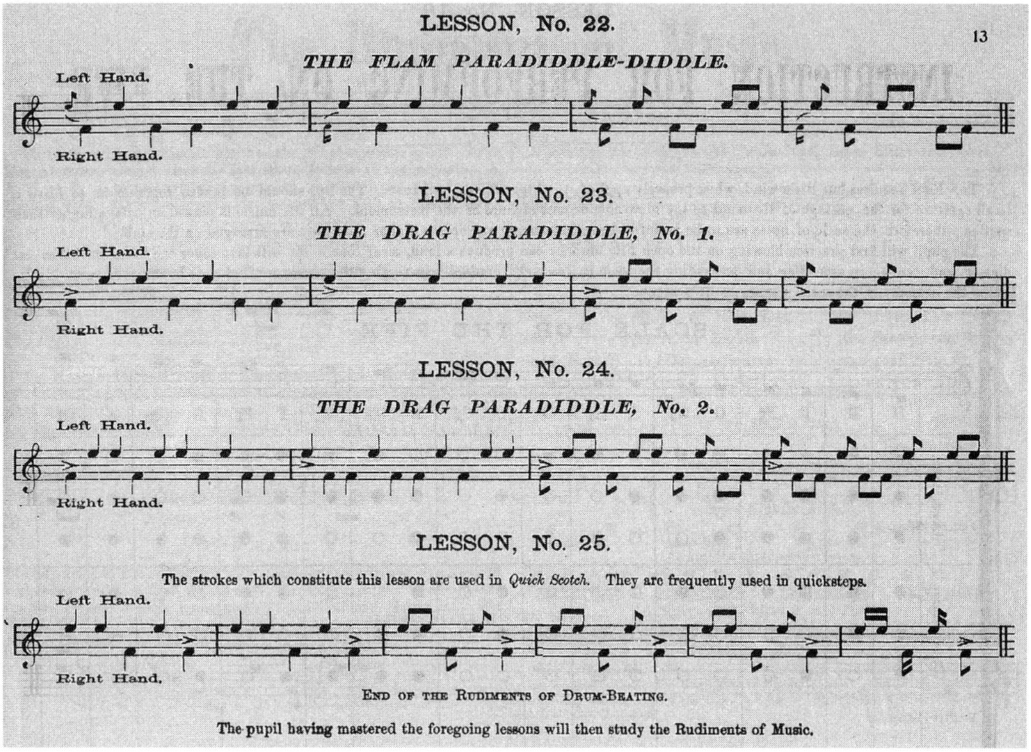

This page of rudiments from the Strube manual shows the lack of a rhythmic notation; only sticking and accents are given. The "Lesson, No. 25" is not given a name; for generations drummers have called it "the lesson 25." In the Ashworth manual (1812) this rudiment is known as the "preparative"; in the oral tradition of the old Connecticut River valley drummers it was called the "firing stroke." Photo in author's collection

or a "flat" flam (in which both sticks hit simultaneously, making a dull popping sound on the drum) would be cause to take off one "tick," or point.

The corps that lacked a "scientific" teacher such as Burns Moore or Earl Sturtze prepared themselves for contests as best they could, but entering a competition was, for many corps, a sideline to their main business, which was to have fun making music together, and to perform at their local Decoration Day ceremonies. The report left by Ed Palmer of the East Hampton corps gives a good idea of the spirit of the corps in those days: "We practiced in our hall once a week, on a Thursday night. We had a time clock [metronome] that we practiced by. When we were going in for competition, we would set the time for 110 beats to the minute and we would try to drum up

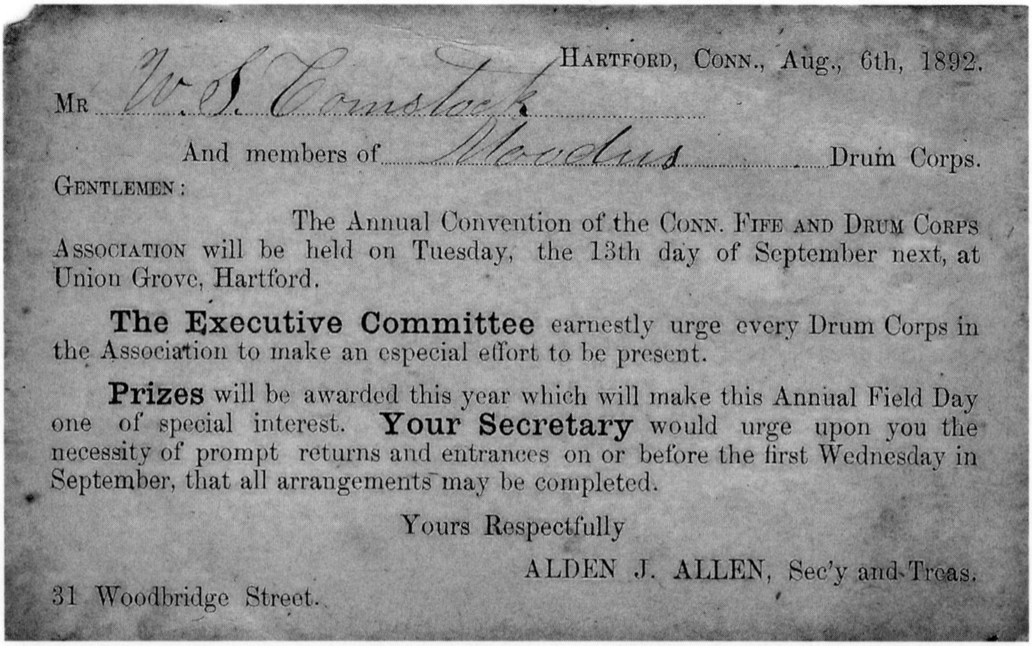
HARTFORD, CONN., Aug., 6th, 1892.

MR W. S. Comstock

And members of Moodus Drum Corps.

GENTLEMEN:

The Annual Convention of the CONN. FIFE AND DRUM CORPS ASSOCIATION will be held on Tuesday, the 13th day of September next, at Union Grove, Hartford.

The Executive Committee earnestly urge every Drum Corps in the Association to make an especial effort to be present.

Prizes will be awarded this year which will make this Annual Field Day one of special interest. **Your Secretary** would urge upon you the necessity of prompt returns and entrances on or before the first Wednesday in September, that all arrangements may be completed.

Yours Respectfully

ALDEN J. ALLEN, Sec'y and Treas.

31 Woodbridge Street.

This penny postcard was sent to the Moodus Corps as notice of and invitation to the 1892 State Convention of the Connecticut Fifers and Drummers Association Reproduced courtesy of Amy Armstrong; photo by Sally Rothenhaus

to this point. It was a lot of fun watching the pendulum go back and forth. It got so, after a while, we would strike a 110 right on the head; not all the time, but every now and then." (How well I know that feeling!) From the inception of the CF&DA to the late 1950s, the Ancient contest continued to consist of these elements, albeit with a constant refinement of precision in the judging process, and some changes reflecting the interests of the membership.

In the late 1920s, junior corps (aged eighteen and below) began to compete. Many of these corps were civic organizations run by parents, many of whom were fifers and drummers themselves. Parochial schools also sponsored corps as activities to build school spirit as well as teach music. (In New Haven there were two St. Francis corps, one a parochial school, the other an orphanage, and in Hartford the Catholic parish of St. Patrick and St. Anthony had a very actively competitive corps. To drum corps buffs of a certain age, the abbreviation OLPH immediately calls to mind the corps sponsored by the Brooklyn (New York) church Our Lady of Perpetual Help. Immigrant groups sometimes sponsored corps, for example the Polish Falcons Social Club in Meriden. Groups that were predominantly Irish, Italian, or Polish were quite common. And by the late 1930s there was a class of "all-girl" corps. In 1940, when a record number of 143 corps belonged to the CF&DA, it was decided that all girls and women, whether they belonged to "feminine" or "mixed" corps, would compete in the feminine class for individual awards. It was assumed at first that the girls and women would be at a disadvantage competing against the boys and men. Paul Cormier, eight-time senior snare drum champion, likes to make the self-deprecating point that the female class was an excellent idea, because it allowed the men to keep at least some of the trophies for themselves. Paul played for a few years in the St. Paul's Church corps, a Modern corps from Kensington, and his colleague in that corps, Marie Hickey, earned the highest score of the day in individual drumming one year at the State Convention. Because Paul won the male class, not too many people noticed that his victory that year was notably hollow.

The old-style Ancient corps never made too big an impression on the CF&DA. The lower Connecticut River valley was a backwater of old-fashioned Yankee ideas, and the CF&DA was bustling, modern, and competitive. No president of the CF&DA ever hailed from the corps of Moodus, East Hampton, Deep River, Westbrook, or any of the other Ancient towns. And of all the State Conventions after 1885, only three were held east of the river, one in Rockville, far north of the Ancient towns, one in Deep River, and one in New London, a coastal city far from the majority of the CF&DA's member corps.

A question of musical terminology arises when we consider this history of the competitive "Ancient" corps. If the "Ancient" corps active in the CF&DA were not modeled after the early militia drumming and fife repertory, why were they called "Ancient" at all, and why the eighteenth-century costume (admittedly of only the most minimal authenticity)? The answer lies in the context out of which these corps evolved. Compared to the rapidly evolving marching band music of the late nineteenth century, a style most famously embodied in the person and the marches of John Philip Sousa, any military music that was originally designed for the fife and old-style military drums, usually based on old folk tunes, came to be considered "Ancient." By the turn of the twentieth century, the division between Ancient and Modern style was complete. Fifers in the Modern corps tended to play contemporary marches, popular songs, or light classical numbers ("The Stars and Stripes Forever," "The Poet and Peasant"; later "The Bells of Saint Mary's" became very popular). The Modern drummers were using drums tensioned with

City Park fife and drum corps, from Meriden, mid-1930s. Photo in author's collection

Washington Park, Meriden, early 1940s. Photo in author's collection

metal rods rather than rope, which were significantly smaller and higher pitched than the rope drums. (Sherm Carpenter's Eli Brown drum had a head dimension of nineteen and a quarter inches, whereas a Modern corps rod drum might be only fifteen inches.) And the two-stick rudimental bass drum style that had evolved (in which three or four bass drummers followed the snare drum parts and played their full share of paradiddles and flamacues) was replaced in the Modern corps with a single large bass drum, which was decorously and metronomically tapped with a mallet covered with felt and lamb's wool to make a softer effect.

Sousa himself put his name on an 1885 instruction manual, *The Trumpet and Drum*. (The fife was now an altogether unwanted anachronism.) The new style of military music was at last replacing the fife and drum that had signaled troops for centuries, and the fife was finally replaced by the bugle, an instrument even louder than a fife and completely adequate for sounding signals, even when unaccompanied by a drum. The Modern drummers evolved a lighter drumming style that served an accompanying role to the bugle. No longer required to signal throughout the military camp, the drum was now free to develop a delicacy and lightness that was inappropriate in its older military signaling capacity.

The "Modern" corps (which are not the focus of this book) were strongly influenced by Sousa's approach. Although the fife was replaced by the bugle and by band instruments for professional purposes, the Modern fife and drum corps was much less costly to fund than a brass band and became a popular type of amateur civic ensemble. These took advantage of the thousands of fifers who had participated in the Civil War, and dozens of them existed in Connecticut up through the 1960s. Closely related in repertory were the marching bands of various types, which proliferated in the state's small factory towns as well as cities. The Essex Cornet band played at the Westbrook Illumination of 1888. East Hampton also had its N. N. Hill band, which was connected with a local factory. In its early years the CF&DA had a "piccolo and flute corps" category, as well as Modern and Ancient corps. The piccolo and flute with their later design never supplanted the traditional military fife in New England, although in the Irish music, closely related to the New England fife and drum corps in many ways, the traditional fife has almost completely disappeared, replaced by a consort of flutes. Their variety notwithstanding, around the turn of the twentieth century all these types of ensembles were popular community organizations. The Ancient fife and drum corps was only one of several varieties.

As we have seen, the drummers often dominated the sound as well as the organization of the Ancient corps. The difference in drumming style between Modern and Ancient made for a powerful conflict between the two. In the very act of naming the Moodus Drum and Fife Corps, its originators enumerated the instruments in order of importance. But the Modern corps reversed this order. The harmonization of the fifing, so essential to approximating the effect of a Sousa band, would have been drowned out by the big Ancient-style drums, so the Modern corps used the new band drums, which were smaller. (The small sixteen-by-twelve-inch drums, and even smaller drums used by drummer boys, that the government contracted for during the Civil War may well have influenced the band drummers who came after that war.)

The "open" Connecticut style of drumming now had a rival "closed" style. This new style developed in part as a result of the new instruments (smaller drums), the new, fully harmonized marches, and the new tempo (120 beats per minute had become the army quickstep tempo). The closed style was initially not popular in Connecticut, whose Modern corps tended to play the open style, only speeded up, and with thinner textures. But elsewhere in the country this new way of playing developed rapidly, and ultimately it made the open Connecticut style an anachronism.

A brief consideration of these changes explains much about the development of percussion playing in the twentieth century. The smaller, rod-tensioned drums could more easily be kept at a higher tension than the Ancient ones, and this enabled the drummers to rely on a more lively bounce from the drumhead. All sorts of tricky grace note figures that are extremely impractical when using Ancient drums and the large sticks appropriate to them become enticing possibilities with such instruments.

The most famous locus of these new techniques was the circus. Throughout the nineteenth century, the circuses that traveled across the country gradually developed into elaborate spectacles involving exotic and trained animals, gymnastics, feats of daring, and clowns of surpassing artistry, all supported whenever possible by a circus band. Unlike the military drummer, the circus drummer had no rules or rudiments or prescribed beatings that he had to replicate perfectly at each majestic ceremony. The essence of the circus was its sense of wonder and spontaneous excitement, and the drummer's job was to support the acts in the ring with whatever he could think of to enhance the mood. The circus drummers introduced (or disseminated) a new kind of drum roll: instead of carefully playing two strokes in each hand with perfect clarity and evenness, they would "drag" the sticks across the head, bouncing the sticks freely. This "buzz roll," or "press roll," started to usurp the military drummer's open roll as the norm. The ideal of this new type of drum roll was to sound "like tearing a piece of paper." The circus drummers also used rim shots and stick shots (hitting the hoop or rim and the head simultaneously, a sonority long known to military drummers but rarely used).

The closed, bouncing style of drumming was ultimately taken from the traveling circuses into the extremely popular musical vaudeville shows of the early twentieth century. Many of the Modern drummers made a real study of the older military drumming and tried to incorporate elements of it into their new style. Billy Gladstone, the famous drummer at Radio City Music Hall for many years, was well known for his innovation of playing very smooth, seamless buzz rolls and his introduction of techniques using precise, delicate motions with his fingers for fine and very rapid control of the drumsticks. *Buddy Rich's Modern Interpretation of Drum Rudiments*, published in 1942 by the famous New York teacher Henry Adler and still in print, is a trove of extremely difficult combinations of traditional rudiments (much more interesting than the Strube Twenty-Five or the Percussive Arts Society's forty) to be performed with the new "closed," bouncing style. In the Midwest, Charlie Wilcoxon published a series of books of instruction and solo pieces that combine traditional rudiments with the swing rhythms of early jazz and the closed style of the Modern drummers.

The Modern drummers added cymbals to the marching drum sound, both as a steady background wash and as dramatic emphasis at climactic points in the music. The large bass drum gently playing in time with the music's pulse lowered the snare drummer's status still further (in an Ancient corps, the snare drums typically set a tempo with their busier part, not the bass drums, and the drummers' accents, not the cymbal player's, create emphasis). These Modern corps alterations in the hierarchy of percussion are now commonly heard and they all helped to create a new type of drum sound.

In Connecticut, however, the firmly established Ancient style would not be forgotten, and it would strongly influence the development of the Modern style within the state. The Ancients, by the turn of the twentieth century at the latest, had already divided into two; the Ancient corps who played the old style of military music, following Moodus's lead, who saw themselves as custodians of a great American heritage, as much cultural as

The Wilcoxson series of books introduced jazz "swing" rhythms to the rudiments, and Henry Adler's "Buddy Rich" book introduced very difficult variations on the traditional rudiments. Outside Connecticut, the traditional military style came to be replaced by orchestral and jazz drumming. The National Association of Rudimental Drummers included members from all over the United States; it published this collection of solos written by members in 1937. Books from author's collection; photo by Sally Rothenhaus

musical, and the new Ancient corps, intent on developing the more recent styles of the Civil War era but maintaining the fife, the rope-tensioned drum, and usually an eighteenth-century-style uniform, and rejecting the tendency of the Modern corps to abandon the folk music repertory and the open style of drumming.

The Connecticut Drummers

The lingering influence of the militia style of drumming, and the extraordinarily active competitive activities sponsored by the CF&DA resulted in national and even international recognition for the "Connecticut style" of drumming. Because of the interest still shown in this style, and in the drummers who made it famous, I will sketch here some of the principle figures in this development. Over a period of about seventy-five years, from approximately 1885 to 1960, this style was regarded by many as the standard by which other military drumming styles were judged. When the top drummers would play at an individual contest, it was common for 150 or 200 people to gather around the stand to watch them run down rudiments and play their quickstep beatings. As a young drummer whose initial training was from a contemporary school of drumming, I was an observer of the last days of this famous style. Listening eagerly to other drum corps at a parade or a muster, I couldn't help but notice that many of the older drummers moved with athletic ease and smoothness and played with a clarity that I could only envy. At the time, I knew very little about the famous "Connecticut style," but I could easily tell that these drummers knew things about drumming I had not even imagined. And there were a lot of good drummers in those years. At a big muster, dozens of very fine drummers would all be playing the same recognizable style, all knowing the same core repertory of rudiments and beatings. When I was fifteen years old, I was able to begin studying with one of the last, and one of the most knowledgeable, of the Connecticut drummers, Paul Cormier. Without Paul's patience, enthusiasm, and the crystalline perfection of his playing as my model, I would never have become a Connecticut drummer, and would never have learned the history of the term.

The first drummer of national importance to win the Connecticut championship was J. Burns Moore, who had moved to New Haven from Nova Scotia at sixteen, and won the championship in 1891, 1895, 1897, and 1900. Having studied in New Haven with the respected rudimental drummer Jack Lyneham, Burns Moore was able to make a career as a professional drummer instead of staying with the factory work with which most drummers supported themselves and their families. "Kings," Burns Moore is supposed to have said, "could not live a better life." In addition to teaching drum corps (mostly those in the Modern class) Burns Moore also played in the New Haven Symphony, in various dance bands, and for the silent movies, where pianists or small bands complemented the flickering images with tunes and sound effects. According to his obituary, "Back in the years before motion pictures learned to talk, the theater drummer had to be a one-man sound effects crew and Moore was one of the most imaginative and best. One of his more talked-about feats in those days was his creation of the sound of a lion's roar by using a pickle jar with a drum head and a rosined string. The result brought cheers from the audience."

In addition to these more lighthearted activities, Burns Moore taught some of Connecticut's finest drummers, including Bob Redican and Bob

Fig. 6 *Fig. 4* *Fig. 3* *Fig. 5*

LESSON 18 **The Flam Tap**

Start with left stick four inches from pad, right stick straight up, (*Fig. 4*). Strike a light left tap and a right stroke, both sticks striking almost together. Left going up and right going up halfway—(*Fig. 3*), one right stroke leaving sticks in position, (*Fig. 5*). This rudiment reverses. Close and open gradually.

Burns Moore demonstrating the correct sticking of the notoriously tricky flam tap. The correct height of the sticks helped to keep the correct dynamics, but it is quite awkward to learn. Photo by Sally Rothenhaus

VonDeck and he published an instruction book in New Haven in the 1930s called *The Art of Drumming*. In 1954, William F. Ludwig, whose drum company was the country's largest, wrote a new introduction to this book and began publishing it from the company's Chicago headquarters. This book provided all the information a professional drummer of the time required. It teaches reading of standard rhythmic notation, including fairly complicated rhythms in complex and changing meters, well beyond the beginner level. It also explains, with photographs and detailed text, the Connecticut style of drumming used at contests, instructing the drummer as to the exact height of the sticks, and the correct accenting of each of the twenty-five Strube rudiments (plus the single roll). These rudiments were the ones chosen by a group of drummers (including Burns Moore) who formed the National Association of Rudimental Drummers, always closely associated with the Ludwig Drum Company, organized in 1933.

Not every Connecticut champion, of course, made such a successful musical career. It is even possible that some who should have been recognized as champions never were. The case of Sid Basney was brought to my attention by one of Connecticut's very finest drummers, Bob Redican, whom you will soon meet as we consider his own contribution. I had seen a photograph that looked about a hundred years old of a group of African-American men with fifes and drums identified as "The Bolden Corps, Hartford." I asked Redican if he had ever heard of them, and of course he had. Redican referred to the records of individual championships he had collected and pointed out that one of these black men had come in second at the State Convention at least six times between 1893 and 1904 (we don't have any records for three of these years). All of the oldest people I have been able to ask agree with Redican's assessment that the judges would never have given the championship to an African American if they could possibly help it. So second place is on Sid Basney's record for all those years, but many of us think that first place would probably have been the result if the contests had been adjudicated fairly.

The most successful of all the early drumming competitors was Frank Fancher, who won eight of the championships between 1906 and 1924 while playing first with the American Graphophone corps from Bridgeport, then with corps from New Haven, Milford, and Waterbury, and then, moving over to the eastern end of the state, with the Chapman Continentals from Willimantic. Fancher sometimes worked as a fireman, and my friend Kenny Lemley told this story. When Kenny was a little boy, his father, Ed (an avid drummer himself), often took him down to the neighborhood fire station, where Ed would lead drumming sessions. Noticing the enthusiasm of the child, Fancher asked the boy if he wanted to become a drummer. Of course he did. "Watch closely," Fancher said, and he disassembled a rope tension drum, piece by piece, unlacing the thirty or forty feet of rope, removing the leather ears, lifting off the hoops, and, removing the heads and snares, and laid all the pieces out on the floor of the firehouse. "Now, when you put that back together again, I'll give you your first lesson." Kenny got the drum put together and began his drumming life. (When Ed Olsen, historian of the Company of Fifers and Drummers, put this story in print, the child was Kenny's father, Ed. Kenny, always a modest and self-effacing gentleman, always told it to me with himself as protagonist. The point of the story is the same either way.)

Earl Sturtze became the best known of the Connecticut drumming teachers during a teaching career that paralleled the greatest years of activity of

Ginger Ploeger, a fine drummer from the famous Charles T. Kirk fife drum and bugle corps of Brooklyn, New York, competing in individual competition. Earl Sturtze is the judge. Photo in author's collection

the CF&DA, from the 1920s through the 1960s. *The Sturtze Drum Instructor* (1955) illustrated the same approach Burns Moore and countless others had taught but, in an era that glorified mechanization, the movements of the drummer were dictated by the Sturtze system in microscopic detail. For the first time, the placement of each finger on the sticks and the motion of the arms were analyzed in some detail. Sturtze's comment on his photo of the left-hand stick grip gives an idea of the level of detail: "Fig. 1 shows the left hand with the stick held deep in the crotch of the thumb and first finger. The thumb is straight, or nearly so, but not stiff. The end of the first finger is curled slightly over the stick—with the second along the side and slightly above. The last two fingers are held under the stick—almost straight and relaxed. Allow the stick to rest just below the first joint of the ring finger. The little finger is held almost directly under the ring finger." It was important for Sturtze that the drummers not only sound alike but look exactly alike. It is still common to hear among drummers, as an expression of approbation, "he plays like a machine." Teaching hundred of students from the 1920s through the 1960s, Sturtze's system was a modernization of the old militia drummer's style, updated, speeded up, and made to look more strict in its motions. Each tap of each rudiment was prepared by a specific height of the drumstick: unaccented taps were played from three to four inches above the

6

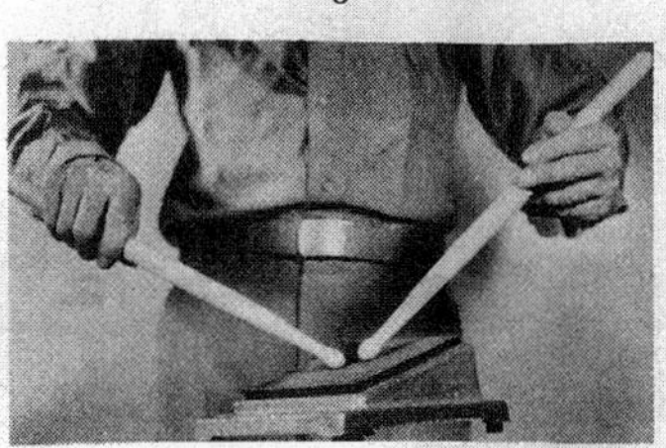

When striking do not hold the hands too high.

7

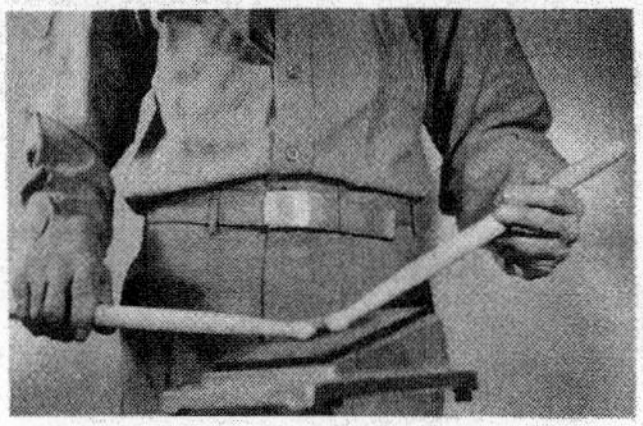

Hold hands low so as to almost strike flat beats.

8

Point sticks forward 45 degrees.

9

10

Keep both wrists turned up in this manner when striking.

11

Both hands forward.

Earl Sturtze demonstrating his relaxed and elegant drumming technique. Reproduced courtesy of Museum of Fife and Drum, Ivoryton, Connecticut

head, accents were played by a full motion of the upper arm, the stick prepared vertically, the hand at eye level. Every rudiment had a precise number of accents (based on the Strube book) and all the other taps were played at precisely the same height.

In practice, the system was considerably more flexible than this explanation suggests, and the effect produced by the best Sturtze drummers was one of extreme gracefulness combined with great power and very considerable speed. The repetition of the fundamental motions for endless hours meant that in a line of drummers trained by Sturtze, the sticks would rise and fall with startling precision. Accented notes or the "attack" of loud rolls were prepared by bringing the sticks up very high, nearly to eye level, and in very good unison. The sound that came out of these drum sections was also very

Bob VonDeck and Bob Redican around 1940, warming up for an individual contest at the Hartford Armory. These were two of the Connecticut drummers who became national champions. Photo in author's collection

uniform. Sturtze spent almost all his time perfecting the technique of the individual student, so each and every drummer in a section was required to play each nuance to Sturtze's satisfaction.

When I started to play in the 1960s, many Sturtze students were still performing. They all had a very smooth motion of their arms, the elbows moving in and out during each roll, the sticks flying up high, effortlessly, as they prepared the attack of the next rudiment. It was relaxed, but very neatly controlled. It was a powerful style, but the soft taps, always played from the four-inch height (something both Burns Moore and Sturtze advocated) precluded any effect of "banging." The limitation of the Sturtze system was that the drummers had a very narrow repertory, based exclusively on the Strube rudiments and their more obvious combinations. The old military drummers' variety of tempi and of musical styles was gone. But technically, it was truly astonishing to see all of these middle-aged men, with their beautiful, graceful way of drumming, marching in parades all over Connecticut, playing with the astonishing ease and clarity that made the "Connecticut Drummer" a phrase with national resonance.

For many years Sturtze taught the St. Francis Parochial School drum corps from New Haven, and both the corps and the individuals he taught were dominant in their classes. Frank Arsenault was the first individual

1938 American Legion National Champion Bob VonDeck. His style, evident in the photograph, testifies to his independence from the regnant Sturtze method. VonDeck's student Paul Cormier says that VonDeck "talked about Moeller and Burns Moore all the time." Photo in author's collection

Sigmond Trybus and Frank Arsenault flank the junior champion, Bob Redican. Arsenault moved to Chicago and became a major influence on the national drum and bugle corps circuit. Photo in author's collection

champion drummer from St. Francis, and he went on to a national career. After World War II, Frank moved to Chicago to take a menial job in the famous Ludwig drum factory on North Damien Avenue and pursued his drumming in this new environment. He soon was hired to teach Chicago-area drum and bugle corps and introduced the Connecticut style. Frank won three national American Legion titles, and his corps, the Skokie Indians and the Chicago Cavaliers, had tremendous influence in the national drum and bugle corps world, establishing a level of precision and elegance that was recognized and imitated throughout the country, particularly in the 1950s and 1960s. Until his death in the mid-1970s Frank continued to tour, giving clinics for the Ludwig drum company, and spreading the Connecticut style around the world.

Most Connecticut drummers stayed in Connecticut, and drumming remained an active hobby for them rather than a profession. The soft-spoken Hugh Quigley, a devoted family man who was present at nearly every Connecticut competition and muster for many decades, was another alumnus of Sturtze's St. Francis drum section. On graduation he joined Lancraft, and won six championships between 1941 and 1953, all while playing with Lancraft. "Quig" was a smooth and natural drummer, always seeming to play well within his abilities, never seeming to exert himself, and thus it could be easy to underrate his skill.

The last time I saw him play seriously was in 1988, at Lancraft's one hundredth anniversary parade and muster. I had heard rumors that Quig was ill, and I was eager to see all the old fellows of the Lancraft corps at their celebration. As they came down the street during the parade, closer and closer to me, Quig, in the drum sergeant's position (the right hand side of the front row of snare drummers), stopped playing and took out a big handkerchief to wipe his face. I noticed that the Lancraft drummers, while very good as always, had probably lost a little of their precision, and probably had indulged in a little pre-parade refreshment. After all, this was their celebration, not a contest. Quig, now putting away his handkerchief, saw me in the crowd and waved to me and smiled as they marched by. "Hi, Clarkie," he called out as they passed. Then he picked up his sticks to play and a minor miracle, if you know your drumming, occurred. Instantly, the drum section sounded again just as they had in their contest years—strong, clean, and inimitably Lancraft. I don't know how he did it, but forty-seven years after winning his first championship, Quig still had the power and control and spirit to corral all those drummers and make them play their best.

Quigley's (and Lancraft's) main competition in the 1950s came from the North Branford corps. In individual competitions, Bob Redican and Howard Kenealy, very different personalities and drummers, were highly respected. Howard was one of the first Connecticut drummers to become interested in other musical styles, and he loved all kinds of bands: military music, jazz bands, novelty acts. He brought some of this variety into his drum solos. New and more complex rhythms and combinations of rudiments that showed an inventive mind filled his solos. He wasn't interested in drumming technique so much as he was interested in music, and he was considered a very different drummer from the other Sturtze students. Sadly, Howie developed very severe arthritis while in his forties and became unable to march, and then even to play.

Howard continued to think creatively about drumming, and when he could no longer play, or even walk comfortably, he would sometimes drive across Meriden to the house of his friend and rival Bob Redican. Redican

Hugh Quigley, in his Lancraft uniform. One of Earl Sturtze's most renowned students, Quig played with the St. Francis parochial schools corps in New Haven. After serving in World War II, he joined Lancraft and won six senior championships. He was an extraordinarily effortless drummer, so it was possible for the uninitiated to underestimate the power and quality of his drumming. Quig loved musters, and well into his sixties he remained a leading player at the late-night jollifications, or "jam sessions," that traditionally end each muster day. Photo in author's collection

told me that "Howie would park in front of the house and honk his car horn until I came out, and he'd hand me the music to some new drum solo he had written, and say, 'tell me what you think of that,' and then he'd drive off again." Redican transcribed some of these pieces in his own careful script, and showed them to me decades later. The pieces show Howard as an independent-minded musician, at home with the idiom of his generation, but obviously searching for new and subtle nuances of the rudimental genre.

I first met Howard Kenealy at the 1973 State Meet, long after he had given up playing. Our great champion of those days, Paul Cormier, had told me "Howard is coming today" with the enthusiasm of a five-year-old announcing Santa Claus. Paul took off to escort Howard across the field, and seemed to be gone an inordinately long time. Finally I looked across the field, and saw Paul standing patiently next to a white-haired, unkempt, overweight man with two canes who was making very, very slow progress across the field. After a while you got used to it. When you walked around at a muster or contest with Howard, you allowed extra time, and you never, ever abandoned him before he got where he was going. There was a strength and gentleness in the great drummer's spirit that compelled you to treat him with a special respect.

I only heard Kenealy play once. He wanted a soda while we were watching corps perform at the Westbrook Muster one August, so we walked over to a soda stand. Howard was standing in line behind me while I got his soda, and I heard him say, teasingly, "How the hell can you play with those goddam toothpicks?" I felt my favorite pair of (irreplaceable handmade) Reamer drumsticks being removed from my back pocket. Howard elbowed his way up to the rough plank that was serving as a countertop and started to play one of his old contest solos. On the one hand, nobody takes my good drumsticks and beats on wooden planks with them. On the other hand, I was watching Howie Kenealy drum. I remained silent, and listened, and learned. If Quigley was like an athlete, strong, smoothly coordinated, all effortless grace, then Kenealy was an artist, adding imaginative little crescendi here and there to emphasize a rhythmic nuance, twisting rhythms slightly out of time to create tension. And his drumming had a terrific swing to it, very much like Ken Lemley's. I thought, here is a drummer who grew up in the age of Gene Krupa. Howie's drumming had that same infectious beat, so typically American. In a couple of minutes it was over. Howard handed me my sticks, which had survived the ordeal, and made no further comment

Howard Kenealy, North Branford senior corps, 1950s. The drum is part of the beautiful set Gus Moeller made for the corps. The large trophy is the Dan English trophy, awarded for many years to the senior snare drumming champion by the Lancraft corps, in memory of Dan English, a champion drummer who died very young. Severe arthritis disabled Howard in his forties, but he retained his keen interest in music and drum corps throughout his life. He was the first of the Connecticut drummers to introduce the rhythmic innovations of contemporary American music into his solos. Photo in author's collection

Howard with Paul Cormier (left), 1980s. Between the two of them, they held the Dan English trophy for fourteen years. Photo in author's collection

Howard Kenealy playing at the Deep River Ancient Muster jollification, late 1950s. Photo in author's collection

about either the sticks or his playing, though I believe he did comment that the price of soda was getting unreasonable. I still use those sticks sometimes when I teach a drum corps, and I wish I could introduce the kids I teach to the great Howard Kenealy, so they could see how drumming should really sound.

Bob Redican, the other dominant drummer from North Branford, was another kind of musician altogether. While Kenealy seems to have been driven by his imagination and love of creativity, Redican's leading characteristic was his concern with the perfection of his performance: not a cold, defensive kind of perfection that merely avoids all possible errors but a positive, exuberant vitality that so far exceeds one's normal expectations for the performance of a typical quickstep drum beating that the informed listener is transported. This sounds hyperbolic, but Redican's drumming had this effect on many other drummers. A couple of years ago I ran into my friend Jim Oblon, the very fine jazz drummer, in a coffee shop. Jim's father, a percussionist and band director, was with him, and I mentioned that I was going to Meriden the next week to visit Bob Redican. "Really?" said Jim's father. "I haven't seen him for years. We used to go to the City Park and watch him practice. There was a little grove where he used to practice, and people would go to the park just to watch him run down rudiments. Even people who weren't drummers would go. It was just amazing."

The newly crowned 1946 state champion, Bob Redican, in the uniform of the Emil Senger American Legion Post fife and drum corps of Seymour, Connecticut. Cocky, intensely competitive, possessed of feline reflexes, Redican took "straight" rudimental drumming to a previously unimaginable level of perfection. A student of Mickey Stefanowicz, Burns Moore, and Earl Sturtze, Redican added his own refinements to the Connecticut style and passed his innovations on to his students, including three-time national champion Charlie Poole and eight-time state champion Paul Cormier, both shockingly good rudimentalists. Redican looked (and sounded) as if he had been born with drumsticks in his hands. Photo in author's collection

Bob Redican looking, as always, confident, as he warms up before a contest. Redican had a strict regimen of preparations for contest playing. The day before each contest he drummed not at all, so as to have fresh muscles and a fresh mind when he went on the stand. Photo in author's collection

After getting a start with local drummer Mickey Stefanowicz, Redican joined the Washington Park junior fife drum and bugle corps in the mid-1930s. Bob says that you would pay Burns Moore a quarter every week at drum corps practice for your lesson, and that his parents bought him his first drum, which he paid off by leaving 50 cents every week at the local music store. Burns Moore taught Redican the fundamentals of drumming technique, and later he studied with Sturtze. Bob didn't see much difference between the two in their approach. He must have had his own ideas about practicing, because his kind of virtuosity is not taught.

Redican's preparatory work was done long before the contest on a rubber practice pad at home. Photo in author's collection

He started competing in 1937, and scrambled to get into the top five. By 1939, he won his first Connecticut championship and placed first in four of the five individual contests that he entered. In all, Bob played in seventy contests between 1937 and 1958. He was disqualified on technicalities four times. He placed second ten times. He won forty-six individual contests, including state, regional, and national championships.

Describing Redican's playing is difficult because it so far exceeds what we mean by the term "good drumming." Most good teachers, whether of violin or piano or drums, will tell you that to develop technique properly, you should move very slowly, coordinating the movements of all the relevant joints and muscles, with a minimum of tension and a maximum of relaxation. In addition, you must listen with full concentration to the quality of the tone you make and its rhythmic placement. If you do all of this very,

very slowly, for a very long time, you will develop great speed, because you will eliminate any unnecessary tension, and thoroughly memorize all the motions. This process, in its essence, is how Asian martial arts are taught, as well as classical violin playing. Redican seems to have internalized this approach with extraordinary thoroughness. He always seems to have extra time to make the complete motion of any rudiment, even when playing very fast. He always seems to play "from the shoulder," with a full arm motion, though he simultaneously has the most delicate control of his fingers on the drumsticks of any rudimental drummer I have heard.

Paul Cormier, who played with Redican at the end of his competitive years, mentions two characteristics of his playing that drummers will recognize. First, Paul always says that Bob seemed to have "rubber wrists." Even at top speed, whether playing a long roll (alternating double strokes: left, left, right, right) or a single roll (alternating single strokes, which is impossible for most of us to get going as fast) Bob's wrists and forearms would make a complete motion. Paul also frequently recounts descriptions of Redican's playing of the ratamacue (a notoriously difficult rudiment to play well). Every moderately qualified drummer can get all the notes in, but the nuance of rhythm and dynamics is lost: it tends to sound almost like a roll. Paul was always in awe of the way Redican's ratamacues, even at top speed, had the same nuances as when he practiced them slowly. To fully appreciate this compliment, I realize, you would have to know how excellently Paul himself has played ratamacues.

Redican stories abound among drummers of his generation, and are instructive in learning which of his values his peers most respected. Harold Green is one of the finest rudimental drummers ever to hail from New York state, and one of the gentlest, friendliest, and best-hearted humans on the planet. Harold's teacher, Nick Attanasio, took him as a teenager to his first contest. Harold, always a cheerful drummer, was bubbling over with enthusiasm. Decades later, Harold told me, "There was a guy over at the end of the parking lot playing a roll. He was out of uniform, just wearing a t-shirt and pants. Gosh, that was a good roll. He kept going into it [speeding up] and he just kept going. I'd never heard a roll so fast! So Nick comes over and I say, Gee, how am I ever going to compete against that guy over there! I never heard a long roll so fast and even. Nick laughed at me! He said, that's Bob Redican, and that's his single roll!"

Bob has lived all of his life in Meriden, working as a fireman for the city. When he was promoted to assistant chief, he decided to give up competitions, because he no longer had adequate time to prepare according to the demanding regimen he had established for himself. However, he continued teaching until he was made chief of the department in the late 1960s. Bob developed a famously large drum line for the Modern corps in Prospect (about eight snare drummers, plus tenor drums, bass drum, and cymbals), and he created the drum line of the Connecticut Yanks Ancient corps of Bristol. Both these corps won many contests under Redican's influence.

Bob attracted the best young drummers. At his last competitive corps, the Modern St. Paul's corps of Kensington, a young drummer named Paul Cormier, just graduated from the junior class, came to play with Bob. Paul, who always says that he would rather have been a baseball player, was dragged into drumming by his father, a fife and drum corps fanatic, who became president of the recently formed Colonel John Chester junior Ancient corps of Wethersfield. Paul's three siblings also played in the corps. On Friday nights, after Paul's father returned from work to their home on Brown Street in Hartford, he would take his son down to the tram station, and they would ride the tram to the Hartford bus station, where they would catch a bus to Manchester, walk a mile or so, and arrive, finally, at the home of Bob VonDeck. One of the most revered Connecticut drummers, VonDeck had been a student of J. Burns Moore, won the American Legion national championship in 1937, and then, it seems, never competed again. But he played in various corps, and he taught. Like many of the old-time teachers, he had a sawhorse with a soft rubber pad mounted on each end. Teacher and student would sit facing each other, with the sawhorse in between, and practice together. Paul remembers that VonDeck was not a showy drummer but was good, accurate, and knowledgeable. He taught Paul the basics of reading as well as the rudiments, and in some detail. VonDeck was very particular that the grace note in each flam be loud enough to be heard distinctly, and spaced a little away from the principal note. This is a very old-fashioned, Ancient way of interpreting the flams—reminding me that both Pete Mietzner and Julian Palmes of the Moodus corps also had strong links to the Manchester area.

When Paul graduated from the junior corps, he was not sure which senior group to join. He went to the Royal Typewriter Corps (although not an employee) because VonDeck was teaching there. But VonDeck was ill, and a substitute teacher was needed. The Royal Typewriter Company paid for an expert New York drum teacher to take the train up from the city every week for rehearsal! Unimpressed by the state of the Royal drummers, he

Paul Cormier, around 1950. Typical of many Ancient competitive corps, the Col. John Chester corps of Wethersfield wore Modern cadet-style uniforms but played rope tension drums. The drumsticks in this photo, with their intricate woodworking, were made by Paul's uncle. Photo courtesy of Paul Cormier

instituted a new test for them. Each one had to play his long roll at full speed on a sheet of paper held stretched out by the teacher. Anyone who relied on too much bounce from the drumhead or who had a clumsy touch wouldn't make the grade.

When Paul started to play with Redican in 1959, the older drummer's perfectionism influenced him. In 1960, Paul won the State Meet, the first of eight such wins over a twenty-one year period. Paul's playing was (and is) characterized by its clarity and relaxed precision. He particularly excels in

In the early 1960s, the St. Paul's Modern fife and drum corps of Kensington featured a drum line consisting of four individual champions: Bob Redican, Paul Cormier, Marie Hickey, and Jack Tencza. Photo courtesy of Paul Cormier

the perfect evenness of his rolls, fast paradiddles, and all grace note patterns. I played in the Connecticut Yanks line with him for a few years, and we all agreed that Paul was the easiest drummer to "match" whom we had ever heard. His timing was completely impeccable, both for the tempo and for the tiniest details of execution. Paul has taught many successful corps in Connecticut and Massachusetts, both senior and junior, Ancient and Modern, contest corps and noncompetitive corps, and as I write this, in 2009, he is building up the Marquis of Granby junior corps from Granby. Starting with a class of beginners two years ago, I have seen them on the street for Memorial Day parade just last weekend, and they are playing as you would expect Paul's students to play, cleanly, correctly, and with enthusiasm.

The Influence of the CF&DA

For nearly a century, the standards set and maintained by the CF&DA were among the highest in the nation. Until the coming of the large urban-based drum and bugle corps, there was no finer way to hear marching music in the United States, excepting the very finest service bands.

The positive side of the CF&DA legacy lies in its adaptation of the old militia music of earlier centuries and the Civil War field music to the new musical world of the late nineteenth- and twentieth-century United States. As the CF&DA musicians brought the clarity and precision of the old military drumming techniques to the smaller drums and quicker tempos of a later culture, a standard of technical excellence was set for drummers not only across the state but nationally. The Ancient class of fifing also served to keep alive a whole body of Irish dance music, as the fifers played the jigs, reels, and hornpipes that were not popular in the culture at large. Just as the fiddle masters of the Irish tradition kept their music alive in emigrant regions, the Connecticut fifers did their share as they presented this legacy to the public in parades and popular contests throughout southern New England.

However, the contests became an end in themselves, and the technical accomplishments of individual players and corps became far more important than the tradition from which they derived. An "Ancient" corps became merely one in which the drummers played rope tension drums and, usually, the fifers played a mixture of Irish dances and popular songs such as "Grandfather's Clock" or the "Mockingbird." Gradually, as the older tradition was forgotten, most Ancient drummers became unable to play any of the old military beatings, and the fifers became ignorant of their instrument's historical repertory and replaced it, mostly, with a handful of old chestnuts and lots of Irish dance music taken from fiddle books rather than the tunes that were traditionally played on the fife. As the fifers imitated the ornamentation and nonstop phrasing of the fiddlers (who don't have to stop for breath) a new type of virtuosity was developed for fifers. By the 1960s, the contest corps were declining in number, and the Connecticut River valley corps were less active than they had been in their heyday of the 1880s through the 1930s. Would there be Ancient corps by the twenty-first century? And, if so, what form would they take? The answer surprised all of us.

5 THE CONNECTICUT ANCIENT CORPS OF MOODUS AND EAST HAMPTON

THE LOWER CONNECTICUT RIVER VALLEY even today consists of small towns interspersed between generous patches of woods, and sheltered from modern life by the river. Crossing the river was not casually undertaken in the nineteenth century, and even today there are only four crossings between Long Island Sound and Hartford. Haddam, Higganum, Deep River, and Westbrook, all on the western side of the river, and East Hampton, East Haddam, and Chester, on its eastern shore, each had an Ancient-style corps that remained largely innocent of the innovations encouraged by the CF&DA. The old style of American militia music was best preserved and popularized by the Moodus Drum and Fife Corps, formally organized in 1860.

The Moodus men (women were not welcomed into the corps until recent decades) had a fructifying effect on the neighboring towns. Chester started its Ancient corps in 1868, Deep River in 1873, East Hampton in 1887, and Westbrook in 1910. Each of these drum corps has its own history, its own stories of success and struggle. I will tell you some of the stories from just two of these groups: first, the originator, the Moodus Drum and Fife Corps, and then my hometown corps, which I know best, East Hampton. I believe these stories will give you a clearer picture of how the old corps were organized and the kind of people who played in them.

For the last few years, I have spent one day every autumn in the Moodus section of East Haddam attending the local drum corps muster. Attendance seems almost mandatory for enthusiasts of the Ancient corps, for the Moodus

The old East Hampton Fife and Drum Corps coming up Main Street in 1920. Tom Hyde, who gave me a few lessons, is the snare drummer in the center of the picture. Photo in author's collection

Perhaps the oldest photograph of the Moodus Drum and Fife Corps, taken in Moodus in the 1860s. Photo courtesy of Amy Armstrong

Drum and Fife Corps has been, since time out of mind, our most direct link to the earliest New England tradition of fife and drum music. Amy Armstrong, a Moodus snare drummer whose grandfather and great-grandfather both played in the corps, allowed me to rifle through her family mementoes of drum corps history, and I lifted out of a box an original copy of the *Massachusetts Collection of Martial Musick*, which figured so prominently earlier in this book. In Moodus, this book, nearly two hundred years old, is not a museum piece, just part of Grandfather's drum corps mementoes. And the Moodus people can really play: they are the embodiment of what we call the "open" style of drumming. The rudiments are clearly defined, every grace note is rhythmically clear, every stroke in every drum roll is placed correctly, the fifes play melodies that have been heard for hundreds of years and are still passed down in the corps from generation to generation. And all this is done at tempos that frequently hover very close to von Steuben's recommended common time tempo of seventy-five steps per minute. Most of the drums the corps uses in parade were made by Eli Brown and his relatives in Bloomfield more than 150 years ago. When played firmly with the appropriately long and heavy sticks that the Moodus drummers favor, the ringing, sustained tone of each drum tap fills up the silence between beats, making sense of the very slow tempi. More than any other group I have seen or heard of, the Moodus Drum and Fife Corps provides a window into the culture and the music of the militia music of the small towns of nineteenth-century New England.

Surprisingly, not everyone appreciates the Moodus Drums and Fife Corps, although there has been increasing interest since the 1976 Bicentennial in authenticity in the early performance practice, uniforms, and marching drill of the earliest American period. Yet almost none of the enthusiasts of this new "authenticity" has shown any interest at all in the Moodus tradition. These enthusiasts prefer to graft musical ideas based on historical research in old military manuals onto the playing styles of today. In part, I think this is because the Moodus sound is disturbing. The Moodus musicians generally make a lot of noise, they march very slowly, and nothing is prettified: the drummers don't hold back, and the fifers do not add sweetening harmonies. The music is heavy and purposive.

An argument I have heard made against the historical authenticity of the Moodus sound is that the Connecticut open style of drumming is not an anachronism so much as a strange local mutation. This is possible, although the argument is usually made with an astounding arrogance. The charge as usually made is that "the Moodus Drum and Fife Corps sounds very different from my corps, so they must be wrong." This is not an attitude that makes for good scholarship or even interesting discussion. The Moodus style and repertory antedate all the innovations of the brass band tradition and of widespread music education. Interestingly, the only other style of military drumming that makes an equal claim for historical veracity is the Fasnacht festival style of drumming of Basel, Switzerland. Despite a complete isolation from each other, these two styles show extensive congruence. But the details of that story are best left for the late-night discussions of old drummers surrounded by whisky glasses, ashtrays, and scraps of old music. In my opinion, the Moodus style is an astonishingly accurate preservation of early martial music. For argument's sake, here is the Moodus drumming lineage: Amy Armstrong is today the drum sergeant of the Moodus corps. Amy's grandfather, John Golet, a fifer and bass drummer in the corps, was the unofficial corps historian. Amy learned to drum from my good drumming friend Dave Pear. Both Amy and Dave, as I know from personal experience, are very good, solid, thoughtful drummers who are extremely concerned to maintain the continuity of the Moodus tradition. Dave learned his playing in the Moodus corps in the late 1950s. His teacher was Julian Palmes, born in 1895, who learned the Ancient style in the Manchester area and then moved to Moodus and played with the corps for nearly thirty years.

Palmes was a caretaker and general handyman who worked for a small factory owner in Moodus. He seems to have been of a type not rare in the small towns of those days: intelligent, curious, and hardworking, he could fix most anything that was broken, and seems to have had a very practical curiosity. For instance, he played and was respected by other drummers over a wide section of the Northeast. (Most of the old-timers I have met remember him.) He taught drumming very thoroughly and clearly, as his student Dave Pears's knowledge attests, and he went deep into his subject, demonstrating to Pear the entire process of producing calfskin drumheads. He also amassed a collection of historical drums from the old militia days. Once a friend went to Julian's home on the morning after a violent thunderstorm and was surprised to see a goodly pile of old militia-style drums piled up. Julian explained that during bad lightning storms he always took his drums out of the attic. If the house was struck by lightning and started to burn, Julian wanted to be sure he could save his drums.

Unlike most drum corps drummers (until the present generation) Julian also had a remarkably good command of standard rhythmic notation. He

Julian Palmes of the Moodus Drum and Fife Corps. Julian played and taught drumming, made his own calfskin drumheads, and collected old militia drums. Photo courtesy of Museum of Fife and Drum, Ivoryton, Connecticut

composed his own drum beatings to such tunes as "Bonnie Blue Flag," "The Arkansas Traveler," and "The Downfall of Paris," among many others. His manuscripts are all extremely neat and accurate, and my drum corps has performed his beatings many times. They work very well, are naturally and smoothly written for the player, and always fit easily with the fife melodies. Julian also made his own drumheads, skinning the calves himself, scraping and curing the hides, and "tucking" the heads onto the flesh hoops as he secured them to the shells.

During much of Julian's tenure with the Moodus corps, its drum sergeant was Pete Mietzner, an avid drummer who, in addition to his Moodus work, formed a group to provide a living representation of the painting familiarly known as *The Spirit of '76*. Pete was very particular about his drums and preferred those of Eli Brown to all others. He attributed his skill to the secure foundation provided by his teacher, Dr. U. S. Cook, with whom he began to study in 1900. Pete was very proud of his ensemble, the "Connecticut Spirit of '76," and he took it to parades and performances all around the East Coast, as far away as Washington, D.C. Pete left home when he

The Connecticut Spirit of '76, Pete Mietzner's "other" drum corps (besides Moodus), played all over the East Coast at patriotic celebrations, bringing their "Continental" style (referring to Washington's Continental Army) to twentieth-century audiences. Photo courtesy of Amy Armstrong

was sixteen to be an apprentice toolmaker; he started this ensemble in 1914, when he was eighteen. Like many of the Connecticut drummers, Pete was never a professional musician, but drumming remained a lifelong passion with him. When Pete played for the nationally respected author, drummer, and percussionist George Lawrence Stone of Boston around 1920, Stone reported that he had never heard drumming that sounded anything like it. Stone was one of the drumming teachers and innovators whose names are still a common reference among percussionists, and was an exponent of the kinds of Modern technique designed for smaller drums. Stone wrote a well-known book of marching cadences for drummers, but he was clearly a drummer of the Modern school of "closed" drumming, the antithesis of Pete's very open style, which was completely opposed to the kind of very finely controlled and rapid wrist and finger motions on which Stone based his technique. I wish that I could have been present at that meeting: the two dedicated drummers together, both so involved with their instruments, and each somewhat incomprehensible, I am sure, to the other.

Like many old New Englanders, Pete Mietzner was not averse to a little versifying, and he has left us a set of couplets to commemorate the importance of the drumming tradition in his life. In his verses he makes references to how the terminology of drumming has changed, and suggests that the Moodus sound is unique. But unique because all other twentieth-century drummers had forsaken the traditional military drumming for more contemporary techniques? Or unique because Dr. Cook made some changes in the traditional style to emphasize Moodus's individuality among the other corps? Drummers will enjoy the continuation of this debate for quite some time to come.

The Spirit of '76, *first exhibited at the Philadelphia centennial exhibition in 1876, is an emblem of the republic of the United States, suggesting the valor and fortitude required for the establishment of the republic. Photo courtesy of Marblehead, Massachusetts, Board of Selectmen*

HOW AND WHERE I LEARNED TO DRUM

'Twas back in nineteen-hundred,
Just fifty years ago,

When first I heard the roll of drums,
And it set my heart aglow.

About eight-thirty in the evening,
if memory serves me right

The moon was shining brightly,
And 'twas a balmy August night,

In a little village called Moodus;
Just a country place remote,

Where ancient drumming reigned supreme
And on history's page it's wrote;

Where rudiments were known as rules
And a piece was called a beat;

A soft pad used while learning,
Where one could not fake or cheat;

Where change-hands wasn't called shivers;
Or a three stroke roll a ruff

Where the men who taught this ancient art,
Were strict and knew their stuff;

Each blow was struck distinctly,
For a rebound did not go;

Each hand was raised to the shoulder
With instructions thus and so.

Rhythm, time and execution
Were drilled into the bone.

And a single drum made music,
When one chose to play alone.

They had a system too, quite unique,
Not found in any book,

'Twas the works of a great musician,
Named Dr. U. S. Cook.

Yes, the style was quite unique indeed
But for all they did not boast,

And eighty years ago and more
'Twas the talk from coast to coast.

So this is where and how I learned to drum
justly proud to say,

This mention made as a matter of fact,
In no conceited way.

—Pete Mietzner, Jan. 17, 1950

Like all of us, Pete had fond memories of performances that he had given, and of the cooperative spirit that pervades the best groups. When his partner drummer in the Connecticut Spirit of '76 died suddenly in 1965 of a heart attack, Pete expressed many of these feelings in a letter he wrote to Paul Meunier, headmaster of Cheshire Academy and an avid enthusiast of rudimental drumming. Pete eulogized his friend in the letter: "I'll tell you Paul, I am just about heartbroken, he was one of the nicest fellows that ever lived and I often said he was a better drummer than me. He was strong and rugged and he could really hit a drum. I remember the morning we paraded in Philadelphia he said now you take it easy Pete, it is a hot day and I am ten years younger than you and I will pour it on. He was always kind and thoughtful and had a heart of gold." He ends the letter by praising the ensemble "Not because I belonged [to it], but the Spirit [of '76] was a nice little outfit and made a hit wherever it appeared, but after all there is an end to all and the Connecticut Spirit of '76 is gone but in this home I will drum as long as I can hold a stick. I am passed 70, and perhaps it won't be long."

Pete's teacher, Dr. U. S. Cook, was one of the original members of the Moodus corps of 1860, taught by Hezekiah Percival, who, as we know, was certified by the militia drummer Samuel B. Wilcox from Middletown back in 1821. (I am told that Wilcox lived in the section of Middletown that is now the town of Cromwell.) Dr. Cook was made the "Leader" of music in the Moodus Corps, always a tribute to a musician's competence, but beyond this we have few details of his drumming career. However, it seems most unlikely that a drummer who learned from Percival and who stayed in the same corps for more than half a century would have been a proponent of great changes. In addition to the famous certificate from Samuel Wilcox, we have other evidence suggesting that Percival was an attentive student. When Col. H. C. Hart, who also studied in Middletown, published his fine drum and fife manual, he included a very common drum beating that has long been known as the "Connecticut Halftime." The Hart manual signals, as far as I know, this beating's first publication. Hart also included a fife tune known as "Bruce's Address," which I haven't seen in any other fife book from the era. Both these pieces are in the Moodus repertory, and I was shown them both by the old-timers when I was young. It seems fairly likely that Percival learned more than the certificate suggests, and that he passed the repertory on to the Moodus Corps.

Of Samuel Wilcox, we know that he was a drum major for the Sixth Regiment of the Connecticut Militia and seems to have come from a martial music family, since two other Wilcoxes also served as drum and fife majors in the Sixth Regiment. The certificate Wilcox presented to Hezekiah Percival identifies the teaching method as completely congruent with the earliest detailed presentation of American military drumming we know of.

The pieces of this puzzle fit together so well, and the story is so well-documented and simple, that I do believe that the Moodus drum corps plays something very, very close to the kind of fife and drum music that would have sounded very familiar to Nathan Hale and General Washington. And so I take the Moodus Drum and Fife Corps very seriously, and have tried to learn what I can from them.

Both Pete Mietzner and Julian Palmes emphasized the same skills and approaches to practicing. They taught the old "rules" of drumming, another name for rudiments, and used the same style we find in the early militia manuals. Many of the beatings and melodies the Moodus corps plays to this day can be found in collections such as the Ashworth manual of 1812 or the *Massachusetts Collection of Martial Musick* of 1818. These are not recent additions to the repertory that are a result of historical research by the members. They are the pieces the corps and its forbears have been playing for about two hundred years.

Pete Mietzner wrote that he learned to play using a drum pad of cloth filled with pine needles. The pine needles make a nice soft bed for the sticks to settle into, providing almost no rebound. The Connecticut style is based on this firm control of every tap in every roll, rather than bouncing the sticks, which is considered cheating. When I started to play with the Moodus drummer Dave Pear, he gave me a drum pad covered with strong cloth, the kind of material you would use for covering a sofa, and it was filled with cloth rags. This is important, Dave said, because you have to be able to play without bouncing the drumsticks. Playing on the large eighteen-inch heads that are common to the Eli Brown drums in the extremely humid summers of Connecticut, the calfskin membrane of the drumheads absorbs a lot of water and offers very little rebound for the drummer. Learning to play on a pad of pine needles is not a fetish but a necessity if you want to sound your best in that weather. (Many contemporary drummers who have never played on humidity-soaked skin heads fail to appreciate the importance of this controlled technique, but it is the foundation of the Connecticut style, because the drummer controls every stroke in every rudiment. Many drummers with whom I have played rely on accenting just the final tap of a roll to make their forte or fortissimo, but a good Connecticut drummer can play all the strokes with almost equal power. This is a defining characteristic of the Connecticut style.)

Like all the other small-town corps, Moodus has had its ups and downs over the years. After having had the good fortune of the Percival brothers' energy and knowledge from the corps' original organization just prior to the Civil War, it was cast into some disarray by problems in 1887, and a new constitution was prepared as the group readied themselves for the 1888 season. Their reconstitution notwithstanding, they were clearly already aware of their rich history. The constitution tells us that the corps' purpose is "To preserve more permanently the name and standing of the Moodus Drum and Fife Corps, whose aim is so widely acknowledged because of the many conquests since its inception in 1860; to maintain the style of martial music incident to Continental [Army] days." More specifically, "The object of this organization shall be to improve its members in the art of Martial Music, to permanently establish and maintain the reputation of said Corps, and to furnish martial music on such occasions as opportunity and the vote of the Corps may suggest."

The corps records of this period reveal the normal vicissitudes of all Connecticut drum corps ever since. Rehearsals were held once or twice a month, more often in preparation for big events, less often when conditions militated against rehearsals. For instance, in the month of March 1888 when the Great Blizzard struck and rehearsal (usually held at the "Stone Store") had to be called off because of the weather, the secretary's monthly report takes the form of doggerel verse.

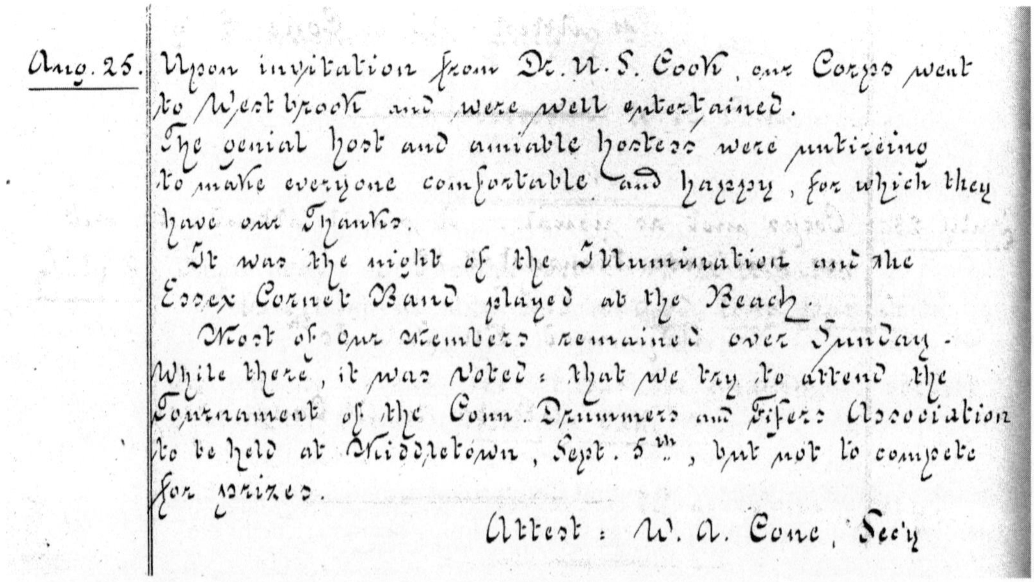

Aug. 25. Upon invitation from Dr. U. S. Cook, our Corps went to Westbrook and were well entertained.
The genial host and amiable hostess were untiring to make everyone comfortable and happy, for which they have our Thanks.
It was the night of the Illumination and the Essex Cornet Band played at the Beach.
Most of our members remained over Sunday. While there, it was Voted: That we try to attend the Tournament of the Conn. Drummers and Fifers Association to be held at Middletown, Sept. 5th, but not to compete for prizes.
Attest: W. A. Cone, Sec'y

The gap between Moodus and the competitive corps is illustrated in this extract from the minutes of a meeting of the Moodus Drum and Fife Corps. The corps voted to attend but not to compete. (The secretary, perhaps intentionally, rearranged the word order of "Connecticut Fifers and Drummers Association.") Reproduced courtesy of Amy Armstrong

Ye Blizzard did roar with a mighty roar
and covered ye Door of ye old "Stone Store"
'Twas blowing and snowing, and the cold was growing
And the saying is true: "what Man proposes
Comes oft to naught for God disposes"!

The corps was more formally organized than many corps of the time: it was incorporated by the state of Connecticut. Proud of this legitimacy and of its written constitution, the corps "voted that the secretary be instructed to have the Constitution of the Corps printed in the 'Ct. Valley Advertiser' and as many copies of same procured and distributed as he thought would be to the advantage of the Corps."

The principal performance opportunities for the corps, then as now, were the parades and public patriotic celebrations at which a historical performance of martial music was appropriate. For instance, on June 2, 1888, when the corps met for practice at a shop owned by one of the members, "A communication was read from the 'Eaton, Cole and Burnham Co.' fire

The Moodus Drum and Fife Corps, now with colonial-style uniforms, probably in the 1880s. Reproduced courtesy of Amy Armstrong

dep't. of Bridgeport, Conn. asking our terms for services July 4th, and we voted to go for $2 each and expenses."

The fire company accepted their terms, and Independence Day of 1888 was celebrated in Bridgeport with eighteen "Continental-style" musicians from Moodus, who reported that it was "A delightful day and a good, long parade!" The $2 each contributed went into the corps treasury, out of which the marchers' expenses were refunded to them. Connecticut drum corps have been funding themselves in this way right up to the present, although now it is rare for a corps to provide expense money except for major trips out of state.

And so it went in small-town America of the late nineteenth century. Dr. U. S. Cook, student of Hezekiah Percival and musical "leader" of the group, invited his fellow corps members to his home (it seems) in Westbrook that August, and the secretary reported, "The genial host and the amiable hostess were untiring to make everyone comfortable and happy. . . . It was the night of the Illumination [fireworks] and the Essex Cornet Band played at the Beach. Most of the members remained over Sunday."

In 1885 the corps performed in Washington, D.C., at the dedication of the Washington Monument. The local anecdote about this event is that they were invited in to the White House to meet President Chester A. Arthur. The president met them in the East Room, where the corps played for him; the thunder of the drums cracked the plaster of the walls. The corps performed for another U.S. president, Benjamin Harrison, at Bennington, Vermont, in 1892. (Apparently the Moodus corps tended to vote Democrat. They played at Harrison's rallies and led a parade in Moodus to celebrate his electoral victory.)

Young Pete Mietzner had joined the group by 1913, when they played at the celebration that opened the East Haddam Bridge, still the only bridge crossing the Connecticut River between Middletown (in the center of the state) and the shoreline at Old Saybrook. (The bridges over the Connecticut River were very important. My aunt remembers the East Hampton corps playing at the opening of the Arrigoni Bridge in Middletown, a few miles upstream from East Haddam, in the 1930s.)

And so the Moodus Drum and Fife Corps continued, marching in parades, performing at patriotic events, training new members to replace the inevitable attrition of the decades. In its organization and its achievements, the Moodus corps is fairly typical of many of the old-time corps that began in the years following the Civil War, however unique Moodus may have been in its repertory. Many other corps played a similar style, and each group had its finest players, who were revered (and who often did most of the work of teaching and organizing the group), and each corps had its own achievements of which its members were justly proud. Most corps did not last as long as Moodus, and most did not have the tradition going back as far as Moodus did with the Percival brothers. To give you a sense of a more typical late nineteenth-century small-town corps, here is an account of the one in my hometown, East Hampton.

In the 1880s, when Connecticut was a thriving industrial region, many towns specialized in a particular product. Thus, among the drum corps towns, Willimantic was the Thread City, Danbury the Hat City, Meriden the Silver City, Waterbury the Brass City, and the Ivoryton section of Essex (named for the exotic tusks used to cover piano keys) specialized in the manufacture of piano actions. East Hampton was the Bell Town. Since the first decade of the nineteenth century, bells of all types and sizes had been made there. After the railroad arrived in the 1860s, both raw materials and finished products could be transported more rapidly, and these businesses grew steadily right up to the Great Depression of 1929. In this area surrounded by forest and with low population density, farming was, of course, also generally practiced, but the main source of income within the town came from the bell factories.

My aunt was born there in 1923, and when I asked her how many people worked in the bell factories, when she was a girl, she seemed surprised that I even asked. "Why, everybody," she exclaimed—with mild exaggeration, as she well knew. For her own father was not a factory worker but a partner in a dry goods store in town—until his partner absconded with all the cash at the beginning of the Depression. After that, my grandfather was a butcher at another local establishment. In all of these aspects—the industrial center, the peripheral services necessary for daily life, the occasional small scandal—East Hampton was typical of the towns in the region. Perhaps our most notable feature, besides the bell factories, was beautiful Lake Pocotapaug with its "twin islands," a recreational focus for the entire town.

As in most small towns in the late nineteenth century, schools consisted largely of one-room schoolhouses (a fine example in our area is still standing on Penfield Hill in Portland). Later, in the new twentieth-century schools, all the students in each grade would still sit together in a single class, learning handwriting, reading, and arithmetic. East Hampton's high school was built in 1939. Before that, students who wanted to extend their education beyond the eighth grade caught a train to Middletown. At the turn of the twentieth century, few made the trip (none of my own grandparents attended high school). A sixth- or eighth-grade education was considered perfectly adequate educational preparation for the life of a working-class man or woman.

In the 1920s and 1930s, music classes or school bands were unheard of. Occasionally an itinerant musician offering lessons found some students, but this was rather haphazard. Anyone who could play and teach music possessed an arcane and highly respected skill, and the opportunity to learn about music was rare enough to have great value. For most men, life's pattern was set by the age of sixteen: they would work forty to fifty hours a week in a mill for as many years as their strength would last, and would hope to marry a local girl and raise children. The women generally planned on being housewives. Travel, art, and education were rare luxuries. Those who were especially interested in them could snatch small amounts as they were available. Some of the townspeople, of course, abandoned all that was familiar and set out, impecunious and ignorant of the world's wicked ways, for the big cities or the West. Those who remained inhabited a working-class world that possessed as much color, excitement, and culture as they could create within the restricted patterns of their lives and imaginations.

Amateur thespians put on plays in church halls and schools; such theatricals were a part of middle-class life throughout the entire nineteenth century. (Jane Austen's characteristically humorous account in *Mansfield Park* illustrates the potential for snobbishness and ego clashes inevitable in these situations.) In the post–Civil War era, even working-class men and women increasingly took part in these productions, and suffered through similarly anguished dramas behind the scenes. Organized team sports were becoming a major part of small-town social life. Football, with its carefully measured field and emphasis on calculated plays, was known as a college boy's sport, and basketball, still in its infancy, could not easily be played without a gym floor indoors or a large paved area outdoors. Baseball, however, well on its way to earning its cognomen "the national pastime," was hugely popular in these years. Professional teams started touring regularly during the 1870s, and East Hampton, like most towns, had its own very amateur group, the Belltown Bombers, competing against teams from other area towns.

There are many similarities between the baseball craze and the popularity of drum corps in Connecticut. In both instances, groups of boys and young men banded together in organized groups and learned a new skill through much repetition during regularly scheduled group practices. Individuals chose (or were assigned) tasks within the organization (bass drummer or fifer, outfielder or shortstop). When practice produced (it was hoped) adequate skill, they donned special uniforms that both set them apart from daily life and identified them as part of their group, and went before the public at specified times and places for (at least) three reasons: to please themselves by using their newly acquired skills, to perform before an audience, and to compete against other groups or teams.

There are differences in emphasis of course: baseball teams have almost no way of showing their skills without competing against others, the public being substantially irrelevant to their success, while the drum corps usually competed only occasionally and played most of the time for their own satisfaction and as an adjunct to patriotic celebrations, which was their primary public purpose. And baseball is physically demanding, making careers relatively short, while fifers and drummers can belong to the same group and participate fully for all their lives.

Although there is some mention of drumming in the town earlier, the organization of the East Hampton Fife and Drum Corps started in the early 1880s when a boy named Clarence Skinner sought out a drum teacher. He found his mentor in Dan Burns, a Moodus drummer who was working at a

On Decoration Day, 1905, the East Hampton drum corps leads a group of veterans up Main Street past the Congregational Church. Photo in author's collection

factory in Leesville, about halfway between the two town centers. Dan was known as a fine drummer and a drum maker as well, and he soon became drum teacher to several of the East Hampton boys. A job was found for him in one of the East Hampton factories, and East Hampton had its first drumming teacher of record. By 1886, the boys had picked up some fifers (only three to start with) and the corps was ready to perform in public.

The drum corps soon consisted of thirty-four members, quite a large number for any Ancient corps. Dan Burns must have had quite a way with young people. Many of the names associated with the corps at that time are still well known to local people: surnames such as Wells, Cavanaugh, Clark, Colbert, Wall, Cahill, Watrous, and Nichols and most of the others are familiar to any East Hampton native. When I took up drumming I was told repeatedly that one of my classmates was the great-grandson of a famous fifer in the corps, Ralph Sellew. This is not such a common family name, and I later found out that Sellew men had been officers in the Sixth Regiment of the Connecticut Militia (a regiment formed with men from our area) back in the 1820s. My classmate, Ralph Phil, now owns a photography business on Main Street in East Hampton. Descendants of several other members of the corps also still live in town or close by.

From the initial group of boys Dan Burns trained (of whom it was later said that nearly all were sons of Union veterans) a second generation of drummers and fifers emerged. The pivotal figure between these two drumming generations was Sherman Carpenter, who grew up surrounded by the excitement of the new local institution. When Dan Burns moved to East Hampton in the 1880s, he took rooms with the Carpenter family, and Sherman Carpenter, then a young boy, became his most widely known and respected student.

Sherm Carpenter (as older residents invariably refer to him) lived in East Hampton all his life; he ran an automotive garage and repair business out of his home. He also made and repaired the drums for the local corps (though I haven't been able to find any of these). My grandfather used to take the family Model T Ford to Sherm's garage (where he kept his drums) for repairs. My father often traveled with him and has told me that Sherm would often hook up a drum and break into a beating in between oil changes or transmission repairs. "Boy, did he make some sound on that drum," my dad says. "I'm telling you, it was loud!"

Carl Price, a summertime resident (and professionally trained church organist) who published a local history of East Hampton (*Yankee Township*), visited Sherm at his home to learn about his peculiar hobby. Price's account records the only meeting I know of between an old-time Ancient drummer and a classically trained musician. The visit took place around 1940, when Sherm must have been in his fifties or early sixties. Sherm first showed off his drum collection (like many drummers, he owned quite a few drums) and was particularly proud of the ones he had made himself, and the two Eli Brown drums that had come to him by way of Moodus and Dan Burns. One had come to Moodus in 1854, purchased by the drummer Frank Brainerd. I surely wish I knew where that drum is now!

At any rate, Sherm sat down, as many older drummers do, and proceeded to play a concert of many drum pieces for his visitor. Price's description of Carpenter is worth quoting at length. A key to the whole session is Price's observation that in Sherm's garage he noticed that "on the table near by rested a copy of *Drummer's and Fifer's Guide* that outlines the intricate and characteristic musical notation used in the higher forms of drumming." This was the Bruce and Emmett manual, which had not been reprinted since 1865, and which indeed does employ an intricate form of notation (each tap of each roll is usually indicated by a grace note, making each page appear very busy). Its presence at this scene suggests, though of course it doesn't prove, two interesting possibilities: first, that Dan Burns had taught Sherm to read music, and second, that the style of "quickstep drumming" that came into fashion with the Civil War was familiar to the East Hampton players. In Moodus, such newfangled ideas were frowned on because the Moodus drummers' mission was strictly to preserve the "Continental" style. Then the concert began:

> Taking off his coat and sitting down to his drum, Sherman Carpenter played for me "Golden Sippers," "The Girl I left Behind Me" [for which Bruce and Emmett has a very nice drum beating], "Sailor's Hornpipe" [virtually the same melody as the "College Hornpipe" I've discussed earlier], "Casey Jones" [surely not a militia music number], "Cuckoo," "Quadrille," "Turkey in the Straw," "Opera Reel," "Quickstep," "1850," [one I've never heard of, though Moodus and the old East Hampton corps had a number called "Forty-Eight" (no one seemed to know the relevance of the title)], and a half dozen other numbers. . . . Once . . . he sang for me "Red River Valley," the while drumming to rhythm. In these various numbers the drummer-artist brought out all the variety of tonal effects possible on an orchestral drum, playing (a) with snares loosened by the pedal [presumably what we call the strainer] (b) without the pedal [muffled drum, without snares?] (c) on the edge of the drum [presumably on the head near the shell where the drum has its most legato, ringing tone] (d) on wood, etc. As for rhythmic varieties—half drag, full drag, ruff, flam, ratamacue, flamacue, compound paradiddles—they were all illustrated in the concert, and more too. . . .
>
> Suddenly, S.C. arose and closed the garage door, to save the neighbors the crash of the finale in his concert. Then, settling down to the Continental drum before him he played in the loudest possible tones "O Dem Golden Slippers," while I whistled the tune out loud. It was a tremendous performance! It seemed to me my teeth were fairly rattling from the vibration: certainly my ear-drums felt as though they were bursting. . . . At the end, the drummer was all out of breath, and perspiration was rolling down his forehead. I asked him if he ever wore out his drumsticks. He replied he is now on his twenty-second pair—he makes his own drumsticks, as well as his own drums. Of course, there had to be an encore to that, and it turned out to be "Dan Tucker," during which the drumsticks now and then flew up in the air and returned to the drummer's hands without disturbing the rhythm one whit.

What can we make of this report? Well, possibly not too much. Carl Price was clearly an enthusiastic and sentimental advocate for East Hampton, the hometown of his wife, who died tragically at a young age, and where he vacationed every summer for decades. He was not a critical audience, and my first response to this account was that Price was merely bandying various percussive terms about at random, but then I decided to look at his comments critically.

Carl Price was a graduate of Wesleyan University in Middletown (B.A. 1902, M.A. 1932), and wrote a number of works on American church music, making him an informed critic of musical performance. His comments are all plausible, and they tell a tale of the gradual evolution of the Connecticut fife and drum tradition. Tunes such as "Casey Jones" and "Golden Slippers" are post–Civil War additions to the repertory, the latter being an extremely popular tune among the Connecticut River valley corps. "The Cuckoo" is probably "Cuckoo Quickstep" or the "Cuckoo's Nest Quickstep," both found in Bruce and Emmett. The names of rudiments Price mentions are found in that manual but mostly not in the older manuals of around 1820. (The question I would love to have answered is this: did Carpenter demonstrate and explain these rudiments to Price, or did Price take a close look at the book and just write them down, assuming that Carpenter was familiar with them all?) The different sonorities Carpenter drew from his drum would have appealed to an organist, for organists tend to think of orchestration or sonority in terms of organ stops. And the parodic prose style Price exaggerates in his description of the "Dan Tucker" finale turns out to be completely reasonable in terms of the traditional drum beating for that number; in its second strain, the drummers traditionally are tacit in measures 2, 4, and 6, so if Sherm had stick tricks worked out, this would have been the piece on which to use them. The volume of a nineteen-inch Eli Brown drum played with the large traditional sticks in a garage would indeed be earsplitting, and other reports suggest that Sherm did like to hit the drum hard from time to time.

Price's question about wearing out drumsticks was an intelligent one. Drumsticks, when sufficiently large and played on calfskin, do not often break, and when they do, it suggests that the drummer is abusing them. But when Price describes the varied sonorities Carpenter used in his drumming, the question comes into focus. In the Bruce and Emmett beating for "The Girl I Left Behind Me," there are indications for hitting the two sticks together, which can damage them, and when Price says that Carpenter

Sherm Carpenter of East Hampton was well known for making and repairing drums as well as for playing them. Photo in author's collection

played "on wood," there are two additional techniques to which he may be referring. Sometimes drummers played on the counterhoops (that hold the head on the shell of the drum). And sometimes they would make a sound like a roll by dragging the right-hand stick across the counterhoop from one side to the other. If the stick is held loosely enough, it bounces over the ropes and clatters onto the counterhoop as it is dragged. Most of the old-time drummers I knew enjoyed this technique, and it is a real trick to get just the right pressure on the stick to make a good roll sound. All of this suggests that Sherm was a pretty avid drummer, who had ventured beyond the Moodus repertory into the fast-paced world of the Civil War–era quicksteps. Carl Price's description of his meeting with "old Sherm" uniquely illustrates the depth of the Connecticut tradition of military drumming.

For most of his adult life, Sherm did not play with the East Hampton corps, or any other, as far as I have been able to ascertain. He wrote no drum book, won no prizes, taught no corps. Yet he was clearly an avid drummer, knowledgeable in the fundamentals of the craft and perhaps an instrument maker as well as a creator of unique beatings (I have no idea what he may have made up for "Casey Jones," although for "Red River Valley" I would be surprised if he didn't use a slight variation of the "Connecticut Halftime" beating (as it is generally known) found in the 1861 Hart manual.

While the East Hampton drummers were very proud of their "once removed" relationship to the Moodus Drum and Fife Corps, through their teacher Dan Burns, certain hints, particularly Sherm Carpenter's Bruce and Emmett manual open on the table, suggest that the newer corps had some slightly more progressive elements in it. The reputation of the Moodus corps has always rested on their strong aversion to anything so up-to-date as Civil War music.

While Sherm didn't perform with the corps, he seems to have stayed on good terms with those who did. Ed Palmer of East Hampton began drumming in 1914 at the age of eighteen, and chose his teacher from among the players in the local corps. His account conveys some of the excitement and dedication involved in producing a good drummer. The lineage of the tradition often seems important to drummers, as it should. Ed was originally attracted by the sound of the drums in rehearsals. His interest was whetted by watching the corps on parade:

> [I was watching] an Old Home Day parade rounding the corner, headed by the East Hampton Fife and Drum Corps. The Corps had six fifers, five snare drummers, two base [*sic*] drummers, and a sensational drum major. The uniforms were of Colonial style, with three corner black hats, blue coats trimmed with red, and brass buttons, and black leggings with brass buttons. Well, this outfit certainly did look beautiful. The impression this corps made on me decided my career then and there. That fall, I went to see George Grover to see about my first drum lesson. Sherman Carpenter was his drum instructor at one time and a former member of

> the Corps. I liked Grover's style of drumming. He was the best and now he was to be my drum instructor. [All quotations from Ed Palmer's accounts are from a memoir held by the Chatham Historical Society.]

First the drummer learns to "run down" the rudiments, progressing from slow to fast. Much repetition is required as the drummer gradually masters the coordination necessary to play them smoothly. Only after the rudiments are mastered up to speed are they combined to make up a whole drum beating, and only at this point does the student begin to play on a drum. Although there were some professional drum teachers, in most towns it was a chance coincidence of mutual enthusiasm, respect, and availability that determined who became a teacher. This was certainly Ed Palmer's experience:

> The instruction method was a very heavy practice pad and a pair of black ebony sticks. I then carried my pad and sticks one mile four times a week for my drum lessons, devoting all my spare time to the practice pad and rudiments. Teacher Grover was rather strict and insisted that certain aspects of the rudiments be mastered before I played on a drum. My progress was advancing very fast. It was in April 1915 that I went to my first Drum Corps rehearsal on Walnut Avenue with my drum instructor, George Grover. Drumming individually before the Corps, they gave me a great hand and said that I was O.K. I was taken in as a member and Oh! how happy I was. My dreams had at last come true.

On entering the army during World War I, Ed was selected as a drummer for his regiment's drum and bugle corps. Returning to East Hampton in 1918, he participated in the corps continuously thereafter, and he took it on himself to train a new generation when the ranks of drummers began to thin during the late 1930s.

One of the drummers who welcomed Ed Palmer into the local drum corps was Tom Hyde. The old English Yankee identity of the town had been altered throughout the nineteenth century by a large influx of Irish Catholics, many of whom had left Ireland at the time of the great famine of the 1840s. The Flynns, Walls, Moriartys, Cavanaughs, and other Irish families based much of their social life around the new St. Patrick's Roman Catholic Church on Middletown Road, and a considerable number of them played in the local drum corps.

Two of Tom's daughters, now in their mid-eighties, recall vividly how important it was for him to attend the weekly drum corps practice. "Oh,

Practicing in the old drum corps hall in the center of town, probably in the 1940s. Photos in author's collection

he never missed that," his daughter Anne says emphatically, for rehearsal night was a social occasion as much as a music rehearsal. Like many fifers and drummers, Tom's interest in music extended beyond the drum corps repertory. His daughters showed me his violin and explained that he tried to teach them to dance a jig and to sing the melody.

They still remember the words to the jig; along with my aunt, they sang them to me some seventy years after Tom had taught them, to the tune of "The Irish Washerwoman," one of the most common jigs among the Irish immigrant community:

Did you ever go into an Irishman's shanty
Where money was scarce and chickens were plenty
The three-legged table was tied to the stool
Did you ever go into Tommy McDoul's?

Tom's daughters believe that he must have been self-taught on the fiddle: "Who could have taught him? There was no one." But I suspect that the story is a little more complicated. Tom moved to New York City once for a few months, taking a course in barbering; and he met his wife while they were both workers at Pratt, Read & Company, which made piano actions down the river in Ivoryton. During one of these youthful adventures he might well have found some musician to teach him the basics of the fiddle. It is true, though, that in East Hampton, violin teachers were as scarce as hen's teeth.

Tom also attempted to teach his children to drum. He would line them up and try to show them the rudiments of drumming. It didn't take. His daughter Yvonne says, "I still remember 'daddy-mammy-uncle-john.' Well, what does that mean?" To a drummer, that means the seven-stroke roll, with one syllable for every stroke on the drum, the rudiment that begins nearly every nineteenth-century military beating. The phrase was one of the onomatopes in the system of mnemonic devices drummers universally used to assist in memorization as far back as, at least, the sixteenth century. Yvonne never learned to play the seven-stroke roll, but she remembered the onomatope.

The fife and drum corps was very largely a social organization, and rehearsals were times to gossip and renew the bonds of friendship as well as review and hone the corps repertory. Membership was also a reason and an opportunity to travel around New England. Tom Hyde's daughters have indelibly planted in their minds the idea that the East Hampton corps once won an award in far-off Saratoga, New York, although the exact nature of the award seems lost in history. What is remarkable now is that during the 1920s or 1930s this group from the Bell Town was able to arrange to travel so far, over 150 miles, in order to perform.

Probably the largest event in which the corps participated was the 1930 American Legion National Convention in Boston. Ed Palmer remembered: "We marched six miles in a never ending line that took nine hours to pass one point. Oh, what a day!"

On occasion, the corps entered the competitions sponsored by the CF&DA. The attitude they took seems refreshingly relaxed. According to Ed Palmer:

> I remember in the early days of the twenties [1920s], [the] Connecticut Fifers and Drummers Association had a competition drumming contest held at Governor's Foot Guard Hall in Hartford. The East Hampton Fife and Drum Corps, organized in 1887 [*sic*], beat out the Moodus Fife and Drum Corps [*sic*], organized in 1860. This was a surprise to every one of the members of the Corps. This was the first time in the East Hampton Fife and Drum Corps' history to bring a first prize silver cup. Judge Von Deck of Manchester said we did it all on our own. It was quite an honor at that time.

I think it likely that the corps won because of Sherm Carpenter's modernizing influence. In those days the contests were largely decided on the basis of which group kept the best time, measured by staying at a steady 110 beats per minute in the Ancient class of competitors. Moodus, of course, kept to the old militia common time step and would have lost by so many points on what we call the "time mark" that the East Hampton corps, playing close to 110, would have won decisively.

The most publicly significant event in the annual calendar was surely Memorial Day, or Decoration Day, as all of the old-timers call it. On May 30 (not the last Monday in May, when the holiday is now celebrated), most of the townspeople would turn out for a parade and the ceremony of laying wreaths and flowers on the graves on the Civil War veterans in the old Lakeview cemetery, overlooking Lake Pocotapaug. The town's dedication to the war had been considerable. Among other contributions, about thirty East Hampton citizens had volunteered together for Company H of the Twenty-first Connecticut Regiment, which fought at Fredericksburg, Drewry's Bluff, and the famous siege at Petersburg, among various other

Old Home Day (shown here: the 1934 parade) has been an important civic tradition in East Hampton for many years, continuing today. Photo in author's collection

actions, mostly in central Virginia near Richmond. During the Petersburg siege, "the Twenty-first were in the trenches when the famous mine explosion was set off near them. Three of them were killed" (Price 1975, p. 191).

All the schoolchildren, grades 1 through 8, were coached by the eighth-grade teacher and principal, Miss Ruth Beckwith, in the correct form for marching in a parade. Looking straight ahead, keeping in time with the drumbeat, the entire student body (about thirty children in each class year) marched in the parade immediately behind the drum corps. Tom Hyde, who worked at the Post Office, close to the school, was given a long lunch hour in the days leading up to the big parade so that he could provide a beat and help teach the children to march in step. The parade, in those days, consisted mostly of the schoolchildren (Boy Scouts were allowed to march separately with their Scout troop) and the drum corps. The route was about two miles long: after the stop at the cemetery the procession continued back to the Congregational Church at the center of town.

After the ceremony on the village green, the fife and drum corps would catch the train to Middletown and march with the veterans groups in the bigger town. As Ed Palmer remembered it, "after Decoration Day services were over in town, we would board the noon train for Middletown. We would parade up Main Street, headed by the boys in blue, the Mansfield Post #53, G. A. R., its fife and drum corps, what they had left out of the war, which was four fifers, three snare drummers and a base drummer. I'm telling you the old fellows could drum 'out of this world.'" (Many GAR posts had fife and drum corps associated with them.)

Although the East Hampton Fife and Drum Corps continued after World War II, interest in the old-time music was waning. And, of course, more and more people were getting jobs out of town. The recruiting and teaching efforts of the late 1930s proved transient. Ed Palmer led the effort, but the battle was lost: "I think we did a swell job [of teaching the new recruits]. With hard work we put it over and I say thanks to my fellow men who especially helped me to make this group of fine young people good fifers and drummers. This corps only lasted a little over a year. World War II broke out, some of the boys went into the Service, some back to college, and so on. It was just too bad." After the war the corps became less active, attracting few new members, and finally became just a memory of the older townspeople.

The story of the East Hampton Fife and Drum Corps shows a pattern that is repeated with local variations throughout the state. Dan Burns, the founder, was an accomplished drummer, and willing to devote a great deal of time and effort to teaching and creating a group. Without his energy, knowledge, and willingness to teach those young people in the 1880s, the group would not have come into existence. Burns was fortunate in being able to attract a critical mass of young people to learn. Without that "dozen or more" boys he would not have created enough social cohesion to maintain the group as a viable enterprise. The town was also at a stage in its development when the drum corps was an important, respected institution. With no music program in the schools, this working-class community showed an appreciation for the music instruction the drum corps provided. The obvious important point in the history of the corps occurred when Burns moved to East Hampton and became more easily available to his students.

But I think the most crucial event came when his landlady's son, Sherman Carpenter, became a serious student. It is such transmission of an oral and aural tradition across generations that enables a folk music to survive free of commercialization. As each generation teaches the next, the tradition continues to live. When World War II interrupted Ed Palmer's and his friends' instruction of a new generation, grave damage was done to the continuity of the tradition.

The corps provided an important element of ritual and color to important patriotic events, and patriotic rituals were becoming increasingly important. It was during the years after the World War I that the Pledge of Allegiance was generally adopted, as the United States became increasingly involved in European and world affairs. Yet the memory of the Civil War was still a living presence for older people. Some Civil War veterans survived, and the memories of that war were still vivid. My great-grandfather was an avid GAR man, and my aunt remembers going to dances in the 1930s sponsored by the Sons of the Union Veterans. Somebody would play the piano, perhaps someone else had a fiddle, and the townspeople would make small financial contributions to the organization and dance late into the night. Many, many people had lost fathers, sons, or uncles in that now distant conflict.

Patriotism and respect for law and order were unquestioned values in small-town life, as was respect for the founding fathers. The three-cornered hats that so attracted Ed Palmer as a young man were an emblem of continuity, of respect for and identification with the generation of Washington, Jefferson, and Adams, just as the marching of the GAR on Decoration Day was a symbol of identification with Lincoln, the president who had consolidated the Union and presided over the eradication of slavery. The history of the United States was, in those years, a more palpable presence, and was viewed with a greater sense of identification than we see today. When the fife and drum corps swung down the street playing the "Battle Hymn of the Republic" or "Rally 'Round the Flag," they were celebrating more than just a band of fellows playing music together; they were celebrating the founding of their nation.

There is a postscript to this account of the East Hampton Fife and Drum Corps that explains a great deal about the way Connecticut's fife and drum tradition has changed since the 1950s. One of the last recruits into the "old corps" was Tom Distefano, who joined his father in the corps during the 1950s, and then joined the army as a drummer. After being discharged, he attended the Hartt School of Music in West Hartford, earned an education

The East Hampton Jr. Fife and Drum Corps, 1965. The adults in uniform were our directors, who marched all our parades with us. Photo in author's collection

degree, and returned to East Hampton as a public school music teacher. It was from Tom Distefano that I (and many other East Hampton children over the years) had my first drum lessons. The East Hampton Junior Fife and Drum Corps was started in 1965, with Tom as music instructor. Jack Paonessa, a local boy who had made good in construction and real estate, was the director of the corps, and Freddy Schluntz, a truck driver new to town, was Jack's assistant. My older brother Tom was a fifer and later the drum major.

My experience in the East Hampton Juniors was very typical of the experience of most fifers and drummers of my generation. My drum lessons were quite successful, because Tom Distefano was a very good drummer. And he became a very good high school band director: affable, talented, properly schooled, and with the natural musician's ability to lead an ensemble. I learned a great deal from him about reading and instrumental technique, how to move naturally when playing, how to rehearse, and what an instrumentalist has to listen for in music. Tom was not a "Connecticut-style" drummer, nor did he have an interest in this curious old tradition. Almost no one did in those days. By the 1960s, the tradition was not considered quaint so much as dangerous.

When public school music programs were still relatively new in working-class towns like East Hampton, the emphasis was understandably put on the skills that went along with "real" music making, not the old-fashioned, out-of-tune shrieking by fifers and the thundering of drummers who played huge, ringing, rope-tensioned instruments with, as was often said, "sticks the size of baseball bats." Most people thought we had moved beyond that old tradition. The young people would be taught to read music, play proper instruments in a proper band, follow the conductor, and play sheet music bought from major publishers. Music was professionalized, and all these things were part of a growing national market for the "music industry," as it was now called. The regional tradition of eighteenth- and nineteenth-century field music was a thing of the past, and we young musicians were to be the future.

My family introduced me to Tom Hyde and Ed Palmer. On the few occasions when I played with Tom and when I watched Ed play at a couple of events, I just didn't know what to make of it. This drumming was so different from what I had been taught that I couldn't really form an opinion about it. They were both extremely nice men, as I remember, and they seemed to see that what we youngsters were being taught was a new world, and they did not push to join in. A couple of other old-timers from the "old corps" did, and it was seldom a happy fit.

We didn't know that we were part of a proud East Hampton tradition, for the old corps had stopped performing before any of us were old enough to have seen them. We just played the music "Mr. Di" gave us to play. By the time I was sixteen, I had gone on to other drum corps activities, and other types of music. I loved being in the drum corps, but there were a lot of things about the mix of old and new that didn't add up for me, and I couldn't put the pieces of this historical mosaic together. That would come later. The link to the past, for me as well as for most kids in Connecticut drum corps in the 1960s, had been broken.

6 THE CONTEMPORARY TRADITION

FOR THOSE WHO BEGAN PLAYING fifes and drums as young people in the 1960s and later, the old reference points of American patriotism and local tradition were weakened by rapid changes in our culture and the increasing geographic mobility of the population. The Vietnam War and the Watergate scandals severely damaged the reflexive patriotism most Americans felt during the New Deal era or during the war against Hitler and the Japanese empire. The increasing dominance of international popular culture accelerated, and constantly improving electronic communications effectively erased long-standing cultural traditions in many parts of the country, especially in areas as densely populated and up-to-date as southern New England. We were much more likely to know the words to Paul McCartney's latest hit than to recognize the melody of a folk ballad such as "Barbara Allen." And a child fascinated by drumming was much more likely to idolize Ringo Starr than the drummers in the local drum corps. School music programs made it easy for children to learn band instruments at very low cost as part of their normal school day. The simple fife or the rope-tensioned drum were no longer inexpensive traditional instruments but anachronistic, unfamiliar objects whose purpose we could not fathom.

So is the history of the fife and drum concluded, and this final chapter merely a requiem for a lost tradition? In some ways and in important ways, I will argue, it is. Yet as I write this, in late May 2009, I have to report that while our fife and drum tradition has drastically changed, it has not yet disappeared. Last weekend, I marched in three Memorial Day parades with my fife and drum corps, the Connecticut Valley Field Music. The previous weekend we had been in Virginia playing a full weekend of concerts and parades to a very receptive audience as guests of the Colonial Williamsburg Fifes and Drums (a very grand group, supported by the Colonial Williamsburg Foundation). Other fife and drum groups from New England and the Midwest joined us marching down historic Duke of Gloucester Street, playing our historical music to an enthusiastic audience. Some of my friends from Massachusetts, the Middlesex County Volunteers, brought their very professional show to Scotland last summer, and for the first time the Edinburgh Military Tattoo, the world's premier military music festival, included American fife and drum music. And in 2010, when the Moodus Drum and Fife Corps celebrates its 150th anniversary, they will cosponsor a fife and drum muster with those new kids the Westbrook Fife and Drum Corps, who will be a mere century old. This doesn't sound like a regional tradition that has disappeared, and it hasn't. But it has changed dramatically, and in this chapter I will try to make sense of these changes.

Many of the changes in our tradition have come from New York, where the old Ancient style was never firmly established. The Moodus Drum and Fife Corps performed in the New York City area as early as 1879, and were very well received there with their unique and powerful sound. A few New Yorkers enjoyed the Moodus approach so much that they formed a corps in Brooklyn called, strangely, Second Moodus, an attempt to imitate the old Connecticut tradition. Ed Lemley, who learned old-time drumming in the Bridgeport Grenadiers, moved to Brooklyn, where he was a blacksmith, and became one of the strongest members of the Second Moodus corps. They say that Ed made a kind of shelf padded with soft rubber that he mounted facing the back seat of his old car, so that when he gave children a ride home after drum corps practice, they could keep drumming on this contraption until they reached their houses. One of these children was his son Kenny, who was to become one of the most respected drum corps drummers of his generation.

Other corps also resisted the modernizing of military music, chief among them being the Veteran Corps of Artillery (V.C.A.; formed in 1790 by veterans of the American Revolution), who performed their field music at regular ceremonial events in the New York area. The V.C.A. always performed on rope-tensioned drums of the smaller, Civil War–era type, and the fifers played a large repertory of quicksteps. Ed Lemley sent Ken all the way into Manhattan so that he could learn to read music from "Cotton-top" McNally, one of the V.C.A. drummers. In addition to reading, Kenny learned a kind of fine control for very quiet playing, which was rare among drummers of his generation. Ken told me that the V.C.A. would perform at very grand balls for the high and mighty of the New York National Guard and other important personages, playing concert pieces while the dance band took an intermission. In these circumstances, playing inside for the white tie and ball-gown crowd, they developed their lighter touch and very brisk tempos. Kenny said they called it "regimental style." A third important New York corps was the Charles T. Kirk Fife Drum and Bugle Corps of Brooklyn. In the 1930s, the Kirks made George T. "Pop" Ripperger their chief musician. He created a strict regimen of hard practice for the unit, and introduced some of the rapid, intricate Irish dance music into the fife section. The corps had a beautiful set of rope-tensioned drums made for them by Gus Moeller. Both Ed and Ken Lemley played with the Kirks, and this highly respected group became a kind of bridge between the Ancient and the Modern corps in New York.

With groups such as the Second Moodus, the V.C.A., and the Kirks preserving the fife and drum repertory and the use of the old-style instruments, the New York area began to develop its own Ancient-style corps, similar to those that participated in the CF&DA. The first great changes in the Ancient corps after World War II came from veterans of this New York fife and drum community, in the form of two very influential corps, the Sons of Liberty and later the New York Regimentals.

The driving force behind the Sons of Liberty was Les Parks, a drummer from Brooklyn who entered the Juilliard School in 1945 after serving with the Coast Guard during the war. During his time at Juilliard, Les started his Ancient corps, the Sons of Liberty, in addition to teaching drum and bugle corps. He is still revered as one of the most influential drummers ever in the drum and bugle corps field, but a great deal of his energy was put into the Sons, where he played with some of the very best drummers, including Bobby Thompson (another musician who became revered in the drum and bugle corps community), Ken Lemley (after he left the Kirks), and the famous virtuoso bass drummer Nick Attanasio.

It is difficult to convey the creative storm the Sons of Liberty brought to the Ancient community. Bill Krug, one of the fifers, composed melodies that fit seamlessly into the style of traditional fife music. These were not fiddle tunes played on the fife or dance music turned into marches, they were marching tunes created for the fife, using the range of the instrument skillfully to project above the sound of the drums, staying recognizably within the bounds of the musical conventions of the old nineteenth-century fife marches, yet individual and energetic. Krug's tunes such as "Devil's Flute" (named for an old soubriquet for the fife), "Yorktown," and "O'Connor's Quickstep"

The Charles T. Kirk Fife, Drum, and Bugle Corps of Brooklyn, New York, made a bridge between old-time "Ancient" military music and the contemporary sound of the military band. Photo courtesy of Museum of Fife and Drum, Ivoryton, Connecticut

*Local newspapers used to be full of short articles and photos about local drum corps. The Charles T. Kirk corps of Brooklyn, New York, was one of the top corps in the Northeast. The beautiful drums in this picture were made by Gus Moeller. (*Left to right: *Ken Lemley, Charlie Riley, Ginger Ploeger.) Photo courtesy of Museum of Fife and Drum, Ivoryton, Connecticut*

The Sons of Liberty on parade, around 1950.
Photo courtesy of Museum of Fife and Drum, Ivoryton, Connecticut

have become as standard for fifers as "Yankee Doodle" or "Grandfather's Clock," and most fifers have no idea that these are twentieth-century tunes. Parks wrote quite creative drum beatings to all these tunes (and many more), juxtaposing rudiments in uncommon ways, creating interplay between the snare and bass drum sections, and generally requiring a level of dexterity that was unheard of in the drum beatings of the day. Parks's compositions for individual contests were considerably more technically demanding than his arrangements for the Sons of Liberty and may fairly be accused of being overwritten. When Paul Cormier first met Parks at an individual contest, he was astonished. He had never seen anyone cram so many rudiments into one solo. And the principle bass drummer of the Sons, Nick Attanasio, was equally influential. Nick, still active in his eighties, was and is a hard hitter and a competitive drummer—competitive to the core. Nick introduced very rapid passages into his solos, and he played with extraordinary power on a bass drum that he kept heavily muffled and tensioned very tight, all of which served to emphasize the clarity and precision of his playing. Nick was clearly determined to make the bass drum repertory just as virtuosic as that of the snare drum, which was a radically new concept.

But many of the innovations of the Sons of Liberty were merely evolutionary progressions of a style that in Connecticut had stopped progressing. For instance, Krug's tunes were not an unheard-of concept: a number of contemporary fife compositions in the 1905 *American Veteran Fifer* also imitate earlier styles while contributing to a new repertory. The same can be said of Les Parks's drum beatings, for even Rumrille and Holton—representing the very first blush of American drumming books—contains uncharacteristically intricate beatings. And in the twentieth century, the midwesterner Charley Wilcoxson had written a number of rudimental "swing"-style drum solos that introduced the syncopated swing style of jazz drumming into the world of rudimental drummers. After the great Chick Webb tore up Harlem in the early 1930s, establishing the drummer as the impetus of a band's energy and the drum solo as the most exciting event in any musical performance, his followers Gene Krupa and Buddy Rich introduced the idea of the long drum solo to a mass (that is to say, white) audience. It was an obvious step for marching drummers to appropriate some of that exuberant virtuosity for themselves.

While the Sons of Liberty were expanding the rhythmic variety of the drum section, another New Yorker was redesigning the fife and its repertory. John McDonagh, a champion fifer from Brooklyn, a decorated combat veteran of the European theater, had returned to New York after World War II with the purpose in mind of creating a fife and drum corps that would equal the best concert bands in musical sophistication and technical excellence. John Philip Sousa had died in 1932, around the time McDonagh began fifing, and the band tradition was nearly as much a part of Americana as the fife and drum corps. When I interviewed McDonagh recently at his eighty-fifth birthday celebration, he told me that much of his inspiration had come from a trumpeter he had met around 1938 who had played in the New York Symphony. John began to transcribe trumpet and cornet solos for the fife, incorporating the very rapid articulations, large leaps, and chromatic runs typical of the virtuoso trumpet and cornet repertory into his individual pieces. I told McDonagh I thought his ensemble, the New York Regimentals, had more of the brightly percussive sound of a brass band than the smoother sonorities of a flute ensemble, and he agreed. "I thought the trumpeter's approach, or the cornetist's, was more brilliant than the flutist's approach to triple-tonguing, or double-tonguing, and that brilliance of sound was what I wanted." While competing in the New York Junior classes in the 1930s (as part of the St. Anselm's parish Modern corps), he began collecting New York state championships, a run he continued in the seniors after the war. He won five championships for Modern fifing and five more in the

The New York Regimental Fife and Drum Band (official name of the corps widely known as the New York Regimentals) performing at the Fairfield muster, around 1960. This group's founder, John McDonagh, wanted to make the fife and drum corps as close as possible to a concert band. He wrote long, thematically integrated medleys of folk tunes, developed an extraordinarily virtuosic fifing style, and required the drummers to learn custom arrangements designed to accompany his fifing. Many of the members continued teaching for decades, spreading McDonagh's "Regimental" style among fifers and drummers. Photo in author's Collection

Ancient class. Undefeated, he told the New York Association officers that he would retire from competition but requested that he be allowed to give an exhibition at each annual championship, for which he would prepare a new virtuoso piece each year. The association refused, and McDonagh always regarded this as a bitter failure for his plan of fifing development.

McDonagh's goal was to create a new type of ensemble: not the traditional fife and drum corps that played historical military music with a greater or lesser degree of authenticity but a fife and drum "band" that would play pieces of Americana, light classical numbers, and traditional airs and dances of Ireland and the British isles arranged into long concert pieces. This was not egomania on McDonagh's part. He believed that the popularity of the traditional fife and drum corps could not survive the shift to the modernity of the postwar era.

By 1947, he had predicted to fellow fifer Ed Olsen that the fife, drum, and bugle corps (such as the famous Kirk group) was obsolete. Bugles would gradually be replaced by horns with valves: essentially, the bugle would become a trumpet. And the fife had too limited a range and inadequate power to compete with a full brass section. The only hope for the fife, McDonagh believed, was to go into the Ancient class and become a piece of Americana. McDonagh's predictions have pretty much all come true. Modern fife and drum corps are now extremely rare. The "straight" traditional bugle is no longer an instrument in drum and bugle corps competitions. But the Ancient corps still exist, in mostly modified form, and McDonagh's aspiration of having a fully chromatic fife that could play fluently in harmony has become the norm among the Ancient corps. No one predicts the future with complete accuracy, but to have made all these predictions at the time he did says a great deal about McDonagh's prescience.

The contest pieces that corps played at this time were, at the most, two or three minutes long. McDonagh wanted to make a repertory appropriate for a whole evening of fife and drum music, in the same way that a concert band would have a varied repertory that would make up a full-length concert. McDonagh created a concert repertory by studying voice-leading and harmony and writing his own fife and drum arrangements, sometimes using familiar square dance tunes ("Chicken Reel," "Devil's Dream"). He also wrote a fantasia on "Yankee Doodle" and, my favorite by far, a medley of Scottish tunes, "Royal Highland Aires." These longer and more formally arranged pieces made other drum corps consider their own repertory more carefully.

Working with instrument maker Roy Seaman, McDonagh redesigned the traditional six-hole military fife, incorporating advances that had been made in the instrument's development. The straight bore, unchanged since Renaissance times, was made conical. This improved intonation, and a wider bore and thicker walls improved the volume of the lower register. The size of the holes was increased, making the fife more sensitive to pitch variation. (If you don't know what you are doing, a McDonagh fife will be more out of tune; if you do know what you are doing, you can play it with more accurate intonation than old fifes.) The most obvious change was that McDonagh added four more finger holes, greatly simplifying the ease of playing pitches that had been virtually unattainable on the old fifes. Various other changes were also effected, transforming the instrument. On this new instrument, the fifer's task was reinvented. With the addition of harmonies to nearly every piece, the ability to control intonation, or being in tune with the other harmony voices, became a primary task. In addition, fifers had always articulated their notes strongly, using a minimum of slurring. The New York Regimentals added the techniques of double and triple tonguing, in the brightly percussive style of the cornet virtuosos of the band tradition, to their standard fifing techniques.

McDonagh's Regimentals could not have existed without the redesigned instrument. He wrote many arrangements in four and even five part harmony for his fife section, as well as passages requiring his fifers to play in unfamiliar keys and to perform chromatic runs that had never been attempted on the old military fife. He transcribed some light classical pieces, including "Carnival of Venice," which Jascha Heifetz made famous in the United States. The goal of the Regimentals was always to transcend the field music and parade tradition altogether and become a legitimate concert band. The ensemble was heavily focused on the fife section, and the drummers, while very good, were only occasionally featured. McDonagh told me that he arranged the drum parts himself, though he would allow the drummers to embellish them somewhat to make them idiomatic for the rudimental style. These drum beatings were often in the style of band drumming, sometimes very sparsely written to allow the busy fife harmonies to be heard. The Regimentals competed assiduously and were undefeated in competitions against all comers in the Ancient class. McDonagh's innovations were clearly dominant.

During the Regimentals run of victories, a new corps was begun in Connecticut that would have an equally large effect on fife and drum music in the late twentieth century, without entering a single competition. Roy Watrous was a short, soft-spoken, and gentle workingman who had grown up as a part of the coastline drum corps community that was largely dominated by the Stony Creek Drum Corps. Organized in 1886, "the Creek" had put their little fishing village on the map for people who loved martial music in the New York and New England region. In this active milieu, Roy's natural musicality developed, and he experimented with woodwind instruments such as the clarinet and the saxophone and nurtured his talent for composing memorable tunes that fit smoothly into the fifing tradition. Many of Roy's tunes were more technically demanding than Bill Krug's, and show the influence of the Irish reel style of nearly continuous rapid scalar and arpeggio patterns. Roy seemed to enjoy putting a little quirk into each tune, and once you start playing them you notice an awkward fingering pattern that he develops in an etude-like way, or a characteristic shift from a minor key to its relative major in the second strain (something not so common in

The Ancient Mariners, founded by Roy Watrous. Audiences loved them for their extraverted performance style; aficionados loved them for their extraordinary repertory. Photo courtesy of Museum of Fife and Drum, Ivoryton, Connecticut

the older Irish tunes), or an awkward leap or rhythmic turn that serves as a unifying motive for the whole tune. In the late 1950s, Roy decided to leave the Stony Creek Drum Corps and started his own corps in the nearby town of Guilford. He assembled there a group of fifers and drummers who would become the most colorful corps in Connecticut, the Ancient Mariners.

Roy was not a domineering character, yet for many years the Mariners developed exactly along the lines of his own musical personality. Roy loved the history of the old colonial period, and he loved the music of the old-time sailors, the jack tars of the square-rigger days, and the fishing men who risked life and limb off the Grand Banks in the great fishing schooners, made famous to generations of schoolchildren by Rudyard Kipling's novel *Captains Courageous.* Bob Ward was the first drum sergeant of the Mariners, and his original drum beatings perfectly matched Roy's fife tunes. The Watrous-Ward collaborations "Drums and Guns" and "Crown Point" have become standards within the fife and drum community, and for good reason.

Scorning the military uniforms and cocked hats of most Ancient corps, the Mariners dressed in seamen's short coats and white duck pants, with tarred round hats. With the swaggering and kilted Babe Kelly swinging a long drum major's mace at the front of the corps, and Roy's nautically derived repertory sounding at a good clip, the Mariners looked not quite piratical but definitely outside the mainstream of good Yankee militia music, and certainly far removed from the kind of pernickety precision that was increasingly the primary concern of the contest corps.

Several of the better New York players, fascinated with the wealth of old-time fife and drum music in Connecticut, as well as by the slower pace of life in the river valley area, moved to Connecticut and joined the Mariners. Ed Olsen from the Sons of Liberty, who had a phenomenal fund of drum corps stories and a memory stocked with dozens of old quicksteps that seem never to have been written down, was one of the first to arrive. Bob O'Brien of the New York Regimentals then came. After the Regimentals retired from competition, two of their snare drummers joined the Mariners, Ken Lemley and Bill Pace. Kenny became the Mariners' chief drummer during many of their formative years, strongly influencing the corps with his extremely musical style. As John McDonagh said of him, "Kenny never wanted to show off. He just came because he wanted to play with the band." This was always Ken's attitude, and every group he played with was improved because his interest in music always came before his interest in drumming.

Bill Gallagher, one of the very best traditional-style fifers, left Lancraft and the competition world for the Mariners. The three McGowan brothers, who came from the Stony Creek Drum Corps, would leave the Mariners intermittently to tour with their very popular club act called the Fabulous Farquahr, featuring folk music and comedy. Frank McGowan was a fifer, his brothers Dennis and Bobby the miracle bass drummers. Whereas Nick Attanasio of the Sons of Liberty had made the bass drum into a virtuoso instrument (an oxymoron if ever there was one) Dennis and Bobby transformed the sound of the bass drum within the ensemble, playing with drumheads so loose that they nearly fell off the drum, whispering their way through quiet sections, and then attacking the fortissimo accents with a full and relaxed arm swing, almost dancing their way through the Mariner repertory. Nick Attanasio made everyone respect the bass drummer. Dennis and Bobby made the bass drum the most entertaining part of the drum corps.

Sonny Lyons, one of the very best of the Sturtze St. Francis corps students, joined and added tremendous strength to the drum section. Sonny was one of the very best of the Connecticut drummers, and even well into his seventies he enjoyed outplaying very fine drummers decades younger than himself. Yet another New Yorker who moved to Connecticut to join the Mariners was Ed Classey. As a boy, Ed's father had worked with Gus Moeller making the famous Moeller drums. Ed was a pure, old-time drummer. He lived carelessly, as several of the Mariners did, drinking a lot, taking carpentering jobs as they came along. He had abandoned drumming for a few decades until he decided to play with the Mariners; he then became the principle composer of the Mariner drum beatings as the corps repertory took shape. He had a pure Moeller approach that he had learned while drumming with Moeller as a child. (The internet and the DVD market are now crowded with "product" claiming to teach the true Moeller Technique. But those of us who played with Ed can compare these new products with something very close to the original.)

Despite the innovations of their musical arrangements, in many ways the Mariners had a rather old-fashioned sound. All through the 1960s they played traditional Crosby model Cloos fifes, with their clear, bright upper register. They played only small sections of harmony, preferring instead the traditional approach, with all the fifers playing the melodies in unison. This was a great boon to the drum section, who could "play out" a little more, not having to worry about "stepping on," or drowning out, the fifers. The drummers acquired the set of drums Moeller had made for a Charles T. Kirk corps of Brooklyn in the 1930s. In short, the Mariners were a very hot group of extraordinarily talented, music-loving men (even today, the Mariners are a male-only group). Even people who thought they didn't like fife and drum music would be drawn to the raw energy of the drumming and the plaintive, folk-like melodies that Watrous (and, I believe, Olsen) frequently contributed to the fife section.

A new type of performance venue contributed to the development of the Mariners and then helped shape many other corps in New England: the drum corps muster. In colonial days, and through the early national period, muster days were set aside for men to gather on village greens and practice their marching drill and musketry. Fife and drum music was a pleasant concomitant to these occasions, but obviously not of primary importance. When drum corps started to get together in the late nineteenth century it was most often for a "field day," or competition. It seems clear that these early competitions were in most (but not all) cases companionable festivals rather than fiercely fought contests. But over sixty years or so of these events, competition changed the nature of fife and drum corps, and a style developed that was primarily based on succeeding within the adjudication system. Yet there were many corps that played, and played well, and looked forward to the opportunity to meet the members of other corps and play without competition.

The Stony Creek Drum Corps on stand at the Deep River Ancient Muster, around 1960. This corps preserved its traditional performance style and repertory for many years after most other corps modernized. Photo courtesy of Museum of Fife and Drum, Ivoryton, Connecticut

Sometime in the 1950s, the Deep River Drum Corps decided to turn their field day into an annual muster. The format would be like that of a field day: the corps would first march in a parade through the main street of the town, and then each corps would play a short concert presentation "on stand" at Devitt Field, where the local baseball diamond was located. Afterward, those who wanted to stay for informal playing or general socializing would be welcome, and the Deep River corps would provide refreshments. By 1960, the Deep River corps had established a tradition that has proved enduring: the Deep River Ancient Muster. The third Saturday of every July, all the Ancient corps are invited to Deep River. Invitations are sent out, but no corps that turns up at the last minute is turned away. Many years, the corps are still going on stand at dusk, after a parade that starts at eleven o'clock or noon, depending on the planning of the Deep River Drum Corps. Because this event is the biggest of the year, many corps from far away plan trips to Connecticut around the third Saturday in July. Corps from the Midwest and even the California Consolidated Drum Band from the San Francisco area have come to play some years. In the late 1960s, one of the famous drummers of Basel, Switzerland, Alfons Grieder, visited the Deep River muster while in America on a business trip. He was bowled over by the similarities of the

The jollification, or "jam session," a tradition of informal, not to say chaotic, playing that traditionally ends every drum corps muster. Photo courtesy of Museum of Fife and Drum, Ivoryton, Connecticut

American corps' playing to the fifing and drumming tradition in Basel. The Swiss Mariners, a brother group to the Ancient Mariners, was soon formed, and various other groups have since organized in Switzerland to play New England–style fife and drum music. The fife and drum groups of Basel have long been fans of the Deep River Ancient Muster, and it is a rare year when at least one group from Switzerland is not present.

Some corps forgo "going on stand" if they are scheduled too late in the day or if the weather is too hot and humid (always a probability in July in the Connecticut River valley), but I was taught as a child that one *always* goes on stand at Deep River, and my compeers in the Connecticut Valley Field Music always plan on making a full day of the muster. You never know what might happen. About ten years ago, we were scheduled to go on very late, so we had time to take a good rest and enjoy the afternoon before climbing back into our fairly authentic wool uniforms and preparing to play. We played a

*The Regimental Fife Club (*right to left*): John McDonagh, Jim Douglass, and Jim McAleney at the Deep River Ancient Muster, late 1950s. They are still using their Cloos fifes; McDonagh's ten-hole fully chromatic fife, made by Roy Seaman, was still in the designing stage. Photo courtesy of Museum of Fife and Drum, Ivoryton, Connecticut*

pretty good show. Shortly after exiting the field a couple of our fifers came up to me and said, "There's some older guy who wants to talk to you about the music." It's not rare, since we play a lot of old-time music, that older musicians approach us to reminisce. This man was a short African American in his seventies with a calm, serious air. He asked me if I had arranged that music. I had. He said that he liked it quite a bit. He spoke generously and appreciatively, but also with a kind of gentle authority that implied that if he liked our performance, he had done at least as well himself, and very often. Or that could be my imagination, because by that point I knew that there was only one person he could be. "Excuse me, sir," I asked, "but are you Jimmy Douglass?"

"Well, yes I am."

In the fife and drum world, receiving a compliment from Jimmy Douglass is roughly comparable to, say, Roger Federer saying something nice about your backhand or Willie Mays telling you you have a good arm. Douglass, a mainstay of the New York Regimentals, is a virtuoso fifer of whom experts speak in the same breath as McDonagh himself, and a fife teacher whose many, many students speak of with reverence and affection. Most important, I had also heard my friend Ken Lemley speak of Jimmy Douglass, not only as a virtuoso but also as one of the real gentlemen of our community. He lives in Georgia now, and we don't see him at many drum corps events. But I met him, and shook his hand, and he listened to my little group, and liked us. And this, ladies and gentlemen, is the reason you should always go on stand at Deep River, even if it is getting dark and the audience is not quite as large as it was at midafternoon.

You can count on seeing most people involved with an Ancient corps at a Deep River muster, and you can be assured that there will be a new music book to buy, antique drums for sale, fife makers plying their trade, and of course fifing and drumming to listen to from Friday afternoon into Sunday. Camping is available for participants, if you get permission ahead of time, and the whole event is run with a wonderfully amateurish devotion. Has there been favoritism to certain corps? Have some folks received the short end of the stick in terms of a time to go on stand, or a bad location in the Sutler's Row, where the marketplace of Ancient accoutrements is found? Well, everybody has a Deep River story to tell of unexpected or unfortunate happenings. But my first Deep River Ancient Muster was in 1964, and I have attended every one since, and I have never gone home feeling it was a wasted day.

The muster isn't just a habit. It is a defining celebration that helps to unite our community. At my first muster and at every one thereafter, I saw the same fellow, a fifer with the Deep River Drum Corps, standing at the edge of the field holding a clipboard, making sure the next corps was ready to play, seeing to it that everything was moving along smoothly. After a few years I learned that his name was Steve Tavernier. Steve was not a star, not a hero, just the guy who stood out in the sun all afternoon, every muster day for half a century and more, just to be sure the muster was a success. After I grew up and became a drumming teacher, Steve drove his son the thirty or so miles from Groton to East Hampton to take lessons from me nearly every Saturday morning for several years. These days I still go to the Deep River muster, and Steve is still standing there with his old-fashioned clipboard, worrying about the length of time each corps is playing, trying to keep the event on schedule.

A couple of years ago, my group was practicing on the Congregational Church lawn, several hundred yards away from Devitt Field. It was very warm and humid. A few corps apparently decided at the last minute that the parade was enough exertion for one day and unofficially dropped out of the program. Well, cellphones started ringing, and our friends came running over to get us; the whole Deep River Ancient Muster was grinding to a halt because the Connecticut Valley Field Music were practicing when they should have been performing. We ran over to the field, carrying our fifes, drums, and flags and moving as fast as our wool coats and pants would let us in the ninety-five-degree heat. When we got to the field, flushed and out of breath, who did I meet but Steve Tavernier with his clipboard, asking me calmly, "Well now, Jimmy, are you ready to go on next?" We did go on, I'm proud to say, and we played all right, given the circumstances.

Many corps started sponsoring musters after the Deep River model. The second longest running muster and always one of the best is the Westbrook Muster, on the fourth Saturday in August, located just a ten-minute drive from Deep River. At Westbrook, the number of corps that play "on stand" is limited (usually to forty-five, still a very large muster), but all corps are welcome to march in the parade. When the Connecticut Valley Field Music started twenty years ago, our first "big" event was the Westbrook Muster parade. There is always a very large and interested audience, almost all the drum corps people attend every year, and all we had to do was fall in line at the back of the parade, after the invited corps, all five of us! We had one fifer (Moodus alumnus John Kalinowski) that day, and four drummers. John performed yeoman work balancing the sound of his fife against all our drums, and two young women who were spectating considered John's valiant efforts and decided that he needed help. One of them, Carol Sullivan, stayed with us for well over a decade, while Jennifer Wick is with us still, as is John, all three having made extremely important contributions to our group. By making their muster parade an open event, the Westbrook drum corps makes it possible for people to meet like this, giving marginal groups and unattached fifers and drummers a chance to be seen, and to experiment with forming new alliances.

All corps give of their best at the Westbrook Muster, but the standout group each year is the Charles W. Dickerson Field Music from New Rochelle, New York. This group exemplifies a great many of the positive qualities of the drum corps world, although they are not from New England, they don't wear period costumes, and they have bugles as well as fifes and drums. In addition, they are an all African-American ensemble.

Their story, as I have it, goes like this. In 1928, an African-American Boy Scout troop was lining up for the Decoration Day parade in New Rochelle.

They were all there, shoes polished and clothes brushed, in line and ready to march, when a parade official came along, and told them to move: "Colored in the back." So they brought up the rear of the parade. Now, one of the parents of those scouts was Gertrude Boddie, and she didn't think much of this. She decided that, next year, the scouts of Troop 16 would be so special that they would get their place at the front of the parade. And they did. A few years later, when they heard about a drummer, an all-around musician who played dances and band concerts and who especially loved drum corps music, they approached him about developing their corps. This drummer loved field music; he made a hobby of visiting veterans hospitals, asking former Civil War drummer boys how they used to play, studying the details of their style by playing with them. Gus Moeller was, in short, what we call a drumming fanatic. And here he was being offered a real challenge: take a troop of boys who knew very little about field music and make them into one of the most respected corps in the Northeast. It was a perfect combination. Moeller taught the drummers, and young Dave Boddie became the drum sergeant, a post he held until his death many decades later. The teacher also made them a set of drums. He taught the fifes a mixture of Civil War quicksteps and more recent tunes that had crept into the repertory by 1930. And he taught the bugle section. The fifes and bugles would alternate rather than playing together. And, the corps went on to march in hundred of parades (and a few contests) thereafter.

The Charles W. Dickerson Field Music normally plays at a good bright tempo, 110 beats per minute or faster, and they play the same repertory Gus Moeller taught them back around 1930, with the kind of vigor and natural ease that only comes from thorough training and utter conviction that one's music is important. The bass drummers play with short, felt-covered mallets, and the large, deep snare drums are completely unmuffled, but played with such refinement that they never drown out the fifes, even if the drums sometimes outnumber them.

A couple of years ago, I sat in the front of the bleachers at the Westbrook Muster, watching the Dickerson corps with a group of my students and their friends, all age fifteen or younger. I wondered if this group of mostly senior citizens playing their old-time music could excite these young people as I had been excited when I first heard them forty-five years earlier. I needn't have been concerned. Class shows, and even young people immured in a popular culture of too many text messages, too many computer games, too much electronically generated music still responded as I had to the natural

The Charles W. Dickerson Field Music, unquestionably one of the grandest parade corps ever. Originally organized as a Boy Scout activity and taught by Gus Moeller, the corps in its second incarnation, shown here, represented the Maceo Bacon Post 2882 or the Veterans of Foreign Wars. Their unique, uninhibited sound is the perfect complement to any summertime social event. Photo courtesy of Museum of Fife and Drum, Ivoryton, Connecticut

Drum section of the Charles W. Dickerson Field Music, showing off the beautiful set of drums their teacher, Gus Moeller, made for them. On the right-hand side of the front line you can see Dave Boddie, one of the truly great gentlemen of American rudimental drumming. Photo courtesy of Museum of Fife and Drum, Ivoryton, Connecticut

energy of the pulsing rhythm and the simple modal melodies. Even young people of the twenty-first century can respond to what Shakespeare identified more than four centuries earlier as "the spirit-stirring drum, th' ear-piercing fife."

As the fife and drum become more and more anachronistic, their preservation becomes an act of cultural will. The world in which all the East Hampton schoolchildren were taught to follow the local drum corps to Lakeview Cemetery on Decoration Day, each child carrying flowers to leave on the veterans' graves, has passed away. The Royal Typewriter factory, where a few workers would gather among the machines after hours, rehearsing their marching music, is no more. The CF&DA contests that used to run until midnight are now over by four o'clock in the afternoon. The factory workers who used to fill the ranks of most corps are gone, along with their factories. Firemen, for some reason, are less likely to be fifers and drummers than in the days of Fancher and Redican, and there are almost no parochial school corps like those that bred Quigley and Arsenault, or McDonagh.

Yet there are groups and individuals to whom this tradition remains important. The Company of Fifers and Drummers, an organization created to foster solidarity among the fife and drum community, holds meetings at its headquarters in Ivoryton, only minutes away from both Deep River and Westbrook. Ed Olsen, the Company's archivist and curator, has created, with a little help from his drum corps friends, an extraordinary collection of antique instruments, music, recordings, and memorabilia documenting the history of the fife and drum corps of the Northeast. For many years Ed indefatigably collected the stories and music that make up the history of our tradition. He eventually became too infirm to continue his researches, but the firm foundation he established will make it easier for others to continue telling the story he cared about so deeply. Ed Olsen died during the week of the 2009 Deep River Ancient Muster. Many drum corps people were in town for his gigantic wake, at which generations of drum corps people paid homage to one of the strongest contributors to our tradition.

A new type of enthusiast has emerged in recent years, much to the surprise of traditional drum corps people. Strangers to us, sometimes from other parts of the country, but often found as parents of young fifers and drummers here in Connecticut, these people see the fife and drum corps as a valuable cultural tradition, and they want their children to know all about it. Now that the fife and drum tradition is no longer a self-evident part of local culture, these people are eager to save it. Some of our junior corps

Ed Olsen just after World War II in the uniform of the Catholic War Veterans. Ed was a Brooklyn boy who loved Connecticut fife and drum corps so much that he moved to Westbrook. His own collection of drum corps history and artifacts became the foundation of Museum of Fife and Drum in Ivoryton, a program of the Company of Fifers and Drummers. Photo courtesy of Museum of Fife and Drum, Ivoryton, Connecticut

still flourish, usually because of the intense dedication of their management. The many, many hours that the directors and parents' committees put into organizing rehearsals, parades, contests, and trips require a real enthusiasm for the task. The music the young people in these corps hear and play is often quite different from the traditional repertory, which has almost disappeared. Most of the well-established junior corps play some variant of a McDonagh-style fife, and consider it normal to play in three- or four-part harmony, avoiding the extreme upper register of the instrument. Fifing is generally less energetic and dance-like and has become more like a flute choir. Drumming, too, has changed. The idea of playing quicksteps at 110 beats per minute with strong rudimental drumming and all the fifes shrieking away in unison is something that is generally left to corps like Stony Creek, Lancraft, and Deep River.

Still, there are musters a couple of times a month throughout each summer, and twenty or thirty drum corps will probably attend any given one of them, many more at Deep River and Westbrook. Massachusetts, our neighbor to the north, which was for a long time moribund in terms of fife and drum activity, is now home to several excellent corps. The Middlesex County Volunteers, headquartered in Medford, is unquestionably the largest and most musically sophisticated fife and drum group now performing; they have a schedule of international trips and a very full calendar of concert and parade performances. Their unique blend of classical-style fifing and

Ed Olsen in one of his many uniforms. No one has done more to preserve the history of the fife and drum in America. Without his indefatigable efforts, we would have little knowledge of this tradition. Photo courtesy of Museum of Fife and Drum, Ivoryton, Connecticut

a constantly changing repertory of musically challenging concert arrangements are represented on a series of eight full-length recordings. Though most people in the Middlesex County Volunteers have only the haziest idea of who John McDonagh is, their group is in many ways a realization of McDonagh's ambitions. Other Massachusetts corps such as the Sudbury Fyfe and Drum Companie and the Lincoln Minutemen are very concerned with capturing the authenticity and historical detail of the revolutionary period.

Each of the principle corps that established themselves after World War II has had musical descendants. The evolutionary approach of the Sons of Liberty and the New York Regimentals has developed into a whole subgenre of its own. John Ciaglia, a young fifer of the Stony Creek corps during the period of the Regimentals, has made the ten-hole fife a lifelong study. His compositions and arrangements, mostly written in a chromaticized version of eighteenth-century counterpoint, assumes that the fife is equally at home in almost any key, and generally eschew the strident tones of the uppermost register of the instrument. This quasi-classical approach is extremely popular with fifers, many of whom now consider drummers merely a necessary evil, covering up the lower register counterpoint with their noise. John Benoit brought the most extreme refinement to the fife's performance technique, playing with a control and precision of intonation more characteristic of classical flute playing than fifing. Skip Healy, a fifer and Irish flute player, has performed on the fife as well as the flute all over America and Europe, playing with an energy and swagger reminiscent of the best old-time fifers, and has become a devoted student and exponent of traditional Irish flute playing. Skip is now a respected fife (and flute) maker, and he has altered the McDonagh chromatic fife to accommodate the preferences of today's top players. All three had long stints in the Ancient Mariners and then broke away to pursue their own musical inclinations; each in his own way has provided a challenge for the next generation of fifers. Among drummers, the direction taken by Les Parks has won the day. Most of our best young drummers have abandoned calfskin heads and traditional rudimental style in favor of the contemporary "marching percussion" approach. The drums are kept so tight that a traditional drum shell will break under the extreme pressure, so many younger drummers prefer multi-ply, factory-made shells to the traditional solid shells of the type Eli Brown and his family made for Connecticut's militia drummers. The traditional rudiments and drum beatings are often treated as beginner music and played carelessly. Many of our finest drummers now aspire to the condition of drum and bugle corps, treating the fife and drum corps, to use a baseball term, as the bush leagues, not nearly so "good" as the giant, vastly funded urban drum and bugle corps.

And then, we also have a small but ardent group of historical enthusiasts, who long for ever greater historical authenticity in music as well as in accoutrements and clothing. Historical research has enabled us to know the music that was played throughout the history of the fifes and drums in much greater detail than did the musicians of only a generation ago, as well as the minutiae of clothing and accessories that were worn or carried. The new hobby of reenacting historical battles and encampments has created a new type of fife and drum enthusiast, the specialist in military music of a specific period. These people are the fife and drum equivalent of the early music specialists in the classical field, and they show a similar dedication to getting each detail exactly right. Their enthusiasm has influenced even those who claim not to care about authenticity. Today, uniforms are generally much more historically authentic, and much repertory (at least for the fife) is being culled from the historical books that remained closed for too long.

There is a palpable enthusiasm at the dozens of events that Connecticut's fife and drum corps attend each year. My own group marches annually in the Ancient musters at Deep River, Westbrook, Marlborough, Moodus, and Lexington (Massachusetts) and at numerous other parades and historical events. We often see the same people, and a mixture of new or unfamiliar faces. We renew old friendships, we listen to the other groups play, and we practice and perform our own constantly evolving repertory of music old and new, a group of people making music together, just for the pleasure of it, just for the sheer joy of being close to "the spirit-stirring drum, th' ear-piercing fife," and letting them sing.

References

Camus, Raoul F. 1976. *Military Music of the American Revolution*. Chapel Hill: University of North Carolina Press.

Davis, Charles Henry Stanley. 1870. *History of Wallingford, Connecticut, from Its Settlement in 1670 to the Present Time Including Meriden, Which Was One of Its Parishes until 1806, and Cheshire, Which Was Incorporated in 1780*. Meriden, CT: published by the author.

Elson, Louis C. 1900. *Shakespeare in Music*. Boston: L. C. Page and Company.

Ewing, George. 1928. *George Ewing, Gentleman: A Soldier of Valley Forge*. Ed. Thomas Ewing. Yonkers, NY.

Fitzpatrick, John C. 1931–1944. *The Writings of George Washington from the original manuscript sources, 1745–1799*. 39 vols. Washington DC: Government Printing Office.

New Grove Dictionary of Music. 1980. 20 vols. New York: MacMillan.

Price, Carl F. 1975 [1941]. *Yankee Township*. East Hampton, CT: Citizens' Welfare Club.

Robinson, Alvan. 1818. *Massachusetts Collection of Martial Musick*. Hallowell, Maine: E. Goodale.

Rousseau, Jean-Jacques Rousseau. 2005. *Confessions*. Trans. Maurice LeLoir. New York: Barnes and Noble.

Sturtze, Earl. 1955. *The Sturtze Drum Instructor*. New York: Schirmer.

Trumbull, Benjamin. 1818. *A Complete History of Connecticut: Civil and Ecclesiastical*. Vol. 1. New-Haven, CT: Maltby, Goldsmith and Co. and Samuel Wadsworth.

Garnet Books

Early Connecticut Silver, 1700–1840
by Peter Bohan and Philip Hammerslough
Introduction and Notes by Erin Eisenbarth

The Connecticut River:
A Photographic Journey through the Heart of New England
by Al Braden

Connecticut's Fife and Drum Tradition
by James Clark

The Old Leather Man:
Historical Accounts of a Connecticut and New York Legend
by Daniel DeLuca

Dr. Mel's Connecticut Climate Book
by Dr. Mel Goldstein

Westover School:
Giving Girls a Place of Their Own
by Laurie Lisle

Crowbar Governor:
The Life and Times of Morgan Gardner Bulkeley
by Kevin Murphy

Water for Hartford:
The Story of the Hartford Water Works and the Metropolitan District Commission
by Kevin Murphy

Henry Austin:
In Every Variety of Architectural Style
by James F. O'Gorman

Making Freedom:
The Extraordinary Life of Venture Smith
by Chandler B. Saint and George Krimsky

Welcome to Wesleyan:
Campus Buildings
by Leslie Starr

Connecticut in the American Civil War:
Slavery, Sacrifice, and Survival
by Matthew Warshauer

Stories in Stone:
How Geology Influenced Connecticut History and Culture
by Jelle Zeilinga de Boer

About the Author

James Clark holds master's degrees from Wesleyan University and from the New England Conservatory of Music, as well as a Ph.D. in Music History and Theory from the University of Connecticut. He has been active in Connecticut's Ancient fife and drum community since 1965, and for the past twenty-one years has been president of the Connecticut Valley Field Music, a fife and drum corps that plays parades and concerts throughout New England. He is also the drum instructor for the Junior Colonials Fife and Drum Corps of Westbrook, Connecticut.

About the Driftless Connecticut Series

The Driftless Connecticut Series is a publication award program established in 2010 to recognize excellent books with a Connecticut focus or written by a Connecticut author. To be eligible, the book must have a Connecticut topic or setting or an author must have been born in Connecticut or have been a legal resident of Connecticut for at least three years.

The Driftless Connecticut Series is funded by the Beatrice Fox Auerbach Foundation Fund at the Hartford Foundation for Public Giving. For more information and a complete list of books in the Driftless Connecticut Series, please visit us online at http://www.wesleyan.edu/wespress/driftless.